The Successful Substitute

How to Prepare, Grow, and Flourish as a Guest Teacher

KIM BAILEY   KRISTEN NELSON

Copyright © 2024 by Solution Tree Press

Materials appearing here are copyrighted. With one exception, all rights are reserved. Readers may reproduce only those pages marked "Reproducible." Otherwise, no part of this book may be reproduced or transmitted in any form or by any means (electronic, photocopying, recording, or otherwise) without prior written permission of the publisher.

555 North Morton Street
Bloomington, IN 47404
800.733.6786 (toll free) / 812.336.7700
FAX: 812.336.7790

email: info@SolutionTree.com
SolutionTree.com

Visit **go.SolutionTree.com/teacherefficacy** to download the free reproducibles in this book.

Printed in the United States of America

Library of Congress Cataloging-in-Publication Data

Names: Bailey, Kim, author. | Nelson, Kristen, author.
Title: The successful substitute : how to prepare, grow, and flourish as a
    guest teacher / Kim Bailey, Kristen Nelson.
Description: Bloomington, IN : Solution Tree Press, 2024. | Includes
    bibliographical references and index.
Identifiers: LCCN 2023042522 (print) | LCCN 2023042523 (ebook) | ISBN
    9781958590614 (paperback) | ISBN 9781958590621 (ebook)
Subjects: LCSH: Substitute teaching--United States. | Substitute
    teachers--United States.
Classification: LCC LB2844.1.S8 B29 2024 (print) | LCC LB2844.1.S8
    (ebook) | DDC 371.14/1220973--dc23/eng/20230920
LC record available at https://lccn.loc.gov/2023042522
LC ebook record available at https://lccn.loc.gov/2023042523

Solution Tree
Jeffrey C. Jones, CEO
Edmund M. Ackerman, President

Solution Tree Press
President and Publisher: Douglas M. Rife
Associate Publishers: Todd Brakke and Kendra Slayton
Editorial Director: Laurel Hecker
Art Director: Rian Anderson
Copy Chief: Jessi Finn
Senior Production Editor: Suzanne Kraszewski
Copy Editor: Evie Madsen
Proofreader: Elijah Oates
Text and Cover Designer: Laura Cox
Acquisitions Editor: Hilary Goff
Assistant Acquisitions Editor: Elijah Oates
Content Development Specialist: Amy Rubenstein
Associate Editor: Sarah Ludwig
Editorial Assistant: Anne Marie Watkins

Acknowledgments

There are many people who made this book possible, but the list begins with Claudia Wheatley. In her effective way, Claudia used her unique charms and influence to challenge us (your coauthors, Kim and Kristen) to write this book. As a result of her successful convincing, we rekindled our past coauthorship, and boy, have we enjoyed the ride! We have had fun learning and growing together. As part of our own learning, we had the chance to connect with many veteran teachers and substitutes who shared their insights. Thanks to the entire Solution Tree Press team and the educators who served as field reviewers—your expertise and knowledge helped us create a better product.

Life doesn't stop when you write a book. We want to acknowledge our families, who showed us patience and understanding when our noses were buried in the computer (even in the midst of the house falling down!). Thank you for all your support and love—you are our solid foundation.

Finally, we acknowledge our unsung heroes in the field of education—guest teachers. Thank you for what you do. We hope this book will be a valuable resource as you serve students!

Solution Tree Press would like to thank the following reviewers:

Tonya Alexander
English Teacher (NBCT)
Owego Free Academy
Owego, New York

Erin Kruckenberg
Fifth-Grade Teacher
Jefferson Elementary
Harvard, Illinois

Shanna Martin
Middle School Teacher &
    Instructional Coach
School District of Lomira
Lomira, Wisconsin

Christie Shealy
Director of Testing and Accountability
Anderson School District One
Williamston, South Carolina

Rachel Swearengin
Fifth-Grade Teacher
Manchester Park Elementary School
Olathe, Kansas

Kory Taylor
Reading Interventionist
Arkansas Virtual Academy
Little Rock, Arkansas

Visit **go.SolutionTree.com/teacherefficacy** to download the free reproducibles in this book.

Table of Contents

Reproducibles are in italics.

About the Authors ix

Introduction 1
    Guest Teacher Mindset 2
    Inside This Book 3
        Chapter 1: Prepare for Success 3
        Chapter 2: Start Out Strong 3
        Chapter 3: Connect With Students 3
        Chapter 4: Make It Manageable and Engaging 3
        Chapter 5: Stay Calm in the Storm 4
        Chapter 6: End Strong 4
        Chapter 7: Thrive and Grow Into Your Future 4
        Chapter 8: Keep Going! Keep Growing! 4

1 Prepare for Success 5
    Get Ready for the Job 5
        Licensing or Certification 6
        Application and Employment Requirements 6
        The Specifics 7
    Create Your Sub Survival Kit 7
    Prepare Your Backup Plans 8
        Read-Aloud Books 8
        Easy-to-Implement Games 10
        Worksheets at a Variety of Levels 11
    Make the Most of Your Resources 11
    Get Ready for the Requests 12
        Learn About the Assignment 12
        Call the Teacher to Get Further Insights 13
        Plan Your Preparation 15
    My Notes and Reflection: Prepare for Success 16

2 Start Out Strong 17
Dress Professionally 17
Arrive Early 18
Check In With the Office 18
Connect With Your Teaching Neighbors 19
Check Out the Room 19
Take a Breath and Get Ready to Greet Your Students 19
Don't Be Afraid to Ask for Help 20
Don't Shy Away From Opportunities to Learn 20
My Notes and Reflection: Start Out Strong 21

3 Connect With Students 23
Be Vulnerable, but Not a Pushover 24
Build Rapport and Trust 24
    Meet and Greet 24
    Let Them Get to Know You 25
    Use Appropriate Humor 25
    Make a Connection to the Learning by Sharing Your Experiences 26
    Acknowledge Each Student 26
    Be Present in the Work 26
Use Engaging Transitions and Routines 27
Incorporate Brain Breaks 28
Create a Collaborative Atmosphere 28
Demonstrate an Inclusive and Respectful Mindset 29
Acknowledge the Regular Teacher's Absence 29
My Notes and Reflection: Connect With Students 31

4 Make It Manageable and Engaging 33
Be a Successful Classroom Manager 33
    Possible Rewards 35
    Management by Movement 37
    Get Students' Attention 37
Address Students Who Don't Meet Your Behavior Expectations 38
Establish Instructional Structures 40
    Full-Class Instruction 40
    Cooperative Groups 41
    Center Rotations in Small Groups 42
    Partner Work 43
    Independent Work 43
Use Strategies for Success 43
    Must Do's and May Do's 44
    Good Questions 44

Table of Contents | vii

    Keep a Notebook to Record Your Learning 45
    Seek Out Instructional Resources 46
    My Notes and Reflection: Make It Manageable and Engaging 47
    I Did Awesome Today! 48
    Super Star Award 49
    Oops, I Didn't Make a Good Decision Today 50

5 Stay Calm in the Storm 51
    Stay Calm and Respond Instead of React 51
        When Concrete Plans Are Lacking. 52
        When Plans Are Unsuccessful or There Are Glitches in Implementation 53
        When Student Behaviors Derail the Lesson. 54
    Reflect on Your Challenging Experiences 58
    My Notes and Reflection: Stay Calm in the Storm 59

6 End Strong 61
    Reflect on What You Learned 61
    Tidy Up the Classroom. 61
    Leave a Note for the Teacher 62
    Check Out in the Office 63
    Care for Yourself 64
        Find Your Own Self-Care Routine 65
        Take Care of Yourself Physically 68
        Take Time Off When Needed 68
        Nurture Your Hobbies and Interests 69
        Remember to Start Fresh Every Day 69
    My Notes and Reflection: End Strong 70
    End-of-Day Report From Your Substitute Teacher 71

7 Thrive and Grow Into Your Future 73
    Preparation Activities 73
    Long-Term Substitute Teaching 74
    Your Teaching Credentials 75
    Sample Résumé and Cover Letter 77
    My Notes and Reflection: Thrive and Grow Into Your Future 79

8 Keep Going! Keep Growing! 81
    Soft Skills Count 82
    Resources to Keep Learning 82
    Enjoy the Ride 84

References and Resources 85

Index 89

About the Authors

Kim Bailey is former director of professional development and instructional support for the Capistrano Unified School District in California. Her leadership was instrumental in uniting and guiding educators throughout the district's fifty-eight schools on their journey to becoming professional learning communities (PLCs). She has also taught courses in educational leadership as an adjunct faculty member at Chapman University in California. Prior to her work in professional development, Kim served as an administrator of special education programs and a teacher of students with disabilities.

Kim's education background spans thirty-eight years, and her work at Capistrano has won national praise. The National School Boards Association (NSBA) recognized Kim's leadership in coordinating and implementing the district's Professional Development Academies. The academies received the distinguished NSBA Magna Award and California School Boards Association Golden Bell Award. Kim has served on the Committee on Accreditation for the California Commission on Teaching Credentialing.

As a writer and consultant, Kim works with educators to build effective leadership in PLCs. She is passionate about empowering teams with practical, collaborative strategies for aligning instruction, assessment, and interventions with the standards so all students receive high-quality instruction.

Kim earned a bachelor of science degree and a master of science degree in education and special education from Northern Illinois University.

To learn more about Kim Bailey's work, visit kbailey4learning (https://kbailey 4learning.com) or follow @Bailey4learning on X (formerly Twitter).

Kristen Nelson is an elementary school principal for the Capistrano Unified School District in California. She has been the principal of several elementary schools, as well as the district's executive director of state and federal programs. Kristen is also a professor at Concordia University, Irvine and teaches leadership courses for the Orange County Department of Education.

Kristen has been instrumental in starting and supporting thriving Spanish dual-language immersion programs and launched the district's fifth language-immersion program at the elementary level. In 2022, the California School Boards Association presented this program with a Golden Bell Award for being an outstanding and innovative program in the state of California. Kristen specializes in working with underrepresented populations in Title 1 schools.

As an educational consultant, Kristen provides support and assistance to education administration programs throughout the state of California. She is a frequent guest lecturer and assists with overall program design. Kristen is the author of several books including *Starting Strong: Surviving and Thriving as a New Teacher*, *Teaching in the Cyberage: Linking the Internet and Brain Theory*, and *Developing Students' Multiple Intelligences*.

Kristen earned a bachelor of science degree in child psychology from the University of California Santa Barbara, where she was also an NCAA Division 1 Women's Basketball player. Kristen also earned a master's degree in education from California State University, Fullerton.

To learn more about Kristen Nelson's work, visit her on LinkedIn (www.linkedin.com/in/kristenjnelson88).

To book Kim Bailey or Kristen Nelson for professional development, contact pd@SolutionTree.com.

Introduction

Welcome to one of the best gigs in existence—substitute teaching! This job allows you to control your schedule, location, the age of students you work with, and the subject matter you focus on—and you'll be home in time to have the afternoon free for your personal hobbies and interests. If the daily grind of sitting at a computer in an office somewhere day after day does not appeal to you, then substitute teaching is an exciting, fun, active, and meaningful way to contribute to students' learning and lives. As a substitute teacher, you can make a difference in the life of a student. There will be a lot of laughter and smiles, as well as a few frowns and tears. Fasten your seatbelt—you're in for a great ride as a substitute teacher!

Most people have memories of substitute teachers from their days as students, and many of these memories are not positive. When you think of your past substitute teachers, you might think of those substitutes who mispronounced student names and gave out a lot of worksheets and busy work as they frequently looked at the clock in the back of the classroom to see if the day was almost over.

However, in contemporary classrooms, substitute teachers are highly valued *guest teachers*, and the increased daily pay rate for substitute teachers in North America is a testament to the growing recognition of the importance of this work. In addition, many North American districts are easing up on their requirements to be a substitute teacher, allowing for more people to enter this exciting role of guest teacher. In a *Time Magazine* article, reporter Katie Reilly (2021) shares:

> Some school districts recently raised pay for substitute teachers to encourage more people to take on the job. The Jordan School District in West Jordan, Utah gave substitute teachers a $7 hourly wage increase and also started offering bonuses of up to $500 depending on how many days they work this semester, the Salt Lake Tribune reported.

This is just one of many districts that increased pay and eased the requirements people need to become substitute teachers. Leaders need, and highly value, guest teachers!

Guest teachers have many responsibilities, with the most important being keeping students safe and continuing the learning even though the regular teacher is absent. The age of silent classrooms is a thing of the past. Classrooms are now full of technology and talkative students working in groups doing hands-on projects. *Substitute teaching* means embracing change and technology, being flexible, and always having a backup plan.

For such a critical job, there are very few books on the market that support and provide practical suggestions and tips for guest teachers. This book is for K–12 substitute teachers who need a guide to grab, read quickly, and gain practical ideas to put into practice immediately. It's meant to support guest teachers as they grow in their profession and support students' social and academic growth. K–12 teachers and administrators might also find this book a valuable tool in their work to support guest teachers.

Guest Teacher Mindset

The best guest teachers walk into the classroom with a strong sense of confidence in their ability to not only control the class but also to offer a unique day for students. They know their areas of strength and always have a plan B in case things go awry. They enjoy students across all grade levels and understand their words can build up students and make a difference in students' lives—even in one day. Whether greeting a group of scared five-year-olds who have never had a guest teacher before or working with a class of high school students who have had many guest teachers in their academic lives, a strong guest teacher can learn to toggle between different age groups and curricula with ease. This is truly a superpower many teachers on staff do not have because they have concentrated on specific grade levels or content areas.

The best substitute teachers are flexible and friendly team players. One longtime popular substitute teacher once shared her secret: "My goal is that every time I leave a school, I want those who work there and go to school there to wish I was permanently on their staff." A successful substitute teacher mindset includes the following qualities.

- Flexible
- Positive
- Focused on growth
- Forgiving
- Engaging
- Respectful
- Empathetic
- Skilled at communication

Inside This Book

This book is organized into eight chapters that walk you through the day of a substitute teacher—from checking in at the office at the very beginning of the school day to checking out at the end. You will find strategies and ideas to make your day flow easily, be productive, and most importantly, be enjoyable. Throughout this book, we (the coauthors) also provide insights from current and former substitute teachers. Their voices of experience are invaluable. Here are some of the things each chapter will address.

Chapter 1: Prepare for Success

Chapter 1 provides organizational tips and helpful information for getting ready to serve as a substitute teacher. The contents address typical paperwork requirements (including a template with questions substitute teachers can use to understand the context of the substitute assignment) and provide recommendations for creating a "survival" kit that includes backup plans and activities to use in a variety of situations.

Chapter 2: Start Out Strong

Chapter 2 provides recommendations and ideas for starting off on the right foot as a substitute teacher, such as suggestions for building connections and proactively setting the stage for positive, professional, and supportive interactions with site leaders, school staff, and fellow teachers.

Chapter 3: Connect With Students

Chapter 3 highlights both the importance of and strategies for connecting with students. From the time students enter the classroom until they leave for the day, how a substitute teacher connects and relates to others can impact students' mindsets about learning. Using scenarios and suggestions from actual substitute teachers and students, this chapter highlights strategies to establish and maintain positive and productive teacher-student relationships while ideally maintaining systems the regular teacher established in the classroom. This chapter also touches on cultural sensitivity and maintaining professional relationships with students.

Chapter 4: Make It Manageable and Engaging

Chapter 4 focuses on classroom-management strategies that ensure the substitute teacher has control of the classroom at all times. It provides ideas on how to set expectations and then reward students for meeting those expectations. It also presents suggestions on how to handle students who misbehave. The chapter then moves on to the most typical instructional structures substitute teachers will encounter or actively plan to use and how they serve to facilitate student learning. Using examples from various grade levels, the chapter illuminates full-class instruction, cooperative groups, center rotations, partner work, and independent work.

Chapter 5: Stay Calm in the Storm

There is a high probability a substitute teacher will experience one of those days when things don't run smoothly. This chapter focuses on strategies to regroup and reset to get back on track, including suggested activities for re-engaging students and guidelines for dealing with different student behaviors.

Chapter 6: End Strong

Chapter 6 provides ideas for debriefing the day's experience and tools and templates for communicating with the regular classroom teacher. We also include a check-out protocol to ensure closure with the front office, and self-care approaches to reflect and renew after a day of substitute teaching, so each day is a fresh start.

Chapter 7: Thrive and Grow Into Your Future

Those serving as substitute teachers may be interested in becoming full-time teachers. This chapter considers and suggests the next steps for either completing the credential process or expanding a part-time role into a full-time teaching position. Chapter 7 provides advice to help professionals continue to grow as substitute teachers (or as future classroom teachers) and includes a sample résumé and cover letter.

Chapter 8: Keep Going! Keep Growing!

This final chapter provides a brief summary of the most important things to remember as a guest teacher, discusses the important skills you gain doing this work, and shares resources to help you continue to grow as an educator.

We are excited you are holding this book in your hands! That means you want to be as prepared as possible to be the best substitute teacher you can be. Thousands of students are waiting for you to impact their lives during this exciting and rewarding adventure.

"Substitute teachers: Because teachers need heroes too!"

CHAPTER 1

Prepare for Success

Some say the road to success is preparation, so this chapter provides some insights and actions you should take before you actually step into a classroom. These actions will help you not only prepare for your assignments as a substitute teacher but proactively help you set the stage for success. This chapter outlines specific actions to help you prepare, including the completion of requirements and paperwork and the organization of materials and resources you can use daily no matter what the situation.

Get Ready for the Job

Before starting any assignment as a substitute, you must ensure your licensing and certification, application and employment requirements, and specific job requirements are in order. Following are some actions to complete. By having everything in order, you'll be eligible to serve as a substitute teacher.

Key Points

- Take time to prepare for your role as a substitute teacher.
- Stay organized and on top of deadlines for licensure, applications, and other requirements.
- Create a "survival" kit to ensure you have what you need, especially when you must improvise.
- Get information about the assignment up front so you can gather grade-appropriate items (such as books and activities) and prepare backup plans.
- Make the most of your human and online resources.

Licensing or Certification

Do you hold the certification or license for the state or school district in which you are seeking a substitute teacher position? What type of position are you qualified to serve? Some U.S. states have specific qualifications for substitute teacher licensing, while other states allow school districts to determine eligibility. For more information about the substitute certification requirements for your state, do a simple internet search (for example: *Substitute teacher requirements for California*).

Note that you'll typically need to renew permits and certificates annually; however, several states are adjusting both their eligibility and renewal requirements, so be sure to research your state. For example, the state of Arizona certifies its substitutes for two years instead of one. Minnesota, on the other hand, has a tiered system with different renewal timeframes ranging from one to five years, depending on the candidate qualifications. Some individuals may reside in an area bordering two states, so it may be advantageous to check into dual certifications.

Once you receive your certificate, make a note of when your permit expires and be sure to start the renewal process two months in advance.

Application and Employment Requirements

Schools generally follow a consistent set of guidelines for their application and screening processes, including their processes for conducting fingerprinting and background checks. Typically, each school district requires a specific application, which applicants complete online. Include all required documentation and check the information you provide (along with your spelling!) before submitting. When a school district asks you to provide your work history or experience, use your most recent information, including an updated résumé that reflects any related work experience. For example, include any prior substitute experiences or experiences in which you worked with school-age children, such as teaching at church, tutoring, or coaching.

As part of the substitute application process, most districts will ask you to indicate your placement or assignment preferences. For example, you will need to indicate whether you are available and willing to serve students at all grade levels or would like to limit your range to the elementary or secondary level. The district may ask if you can serve at all their school locations, which may have travel implications when seeking employment in a large district.

The Specifics

Become aware of the district's pay schedule for substitutes. Some districts vary pay based on the number of days you serve or if you hold a teaching credential. There may be limits on the number of days you serve in a single classroom.

In addition to the pay schedule, become familiar with the system or process the district uses to make substitute assignments. For example, some schools may call you, while others may send information through text or email. Once you are officially hired, many districts provide an email address for substitutes. This allows a substitute to log in to the school's learning network and access online tools and information when subbing. Record this information on your phone so you can quickly access it.

Some districts provide orientation training to review specific guidelines and processes. Be sure to ask whether such an orientation is available and if so, attend.

To continue to be eligible as a substitute or to transition to a full-time teaching position, we suggest the following.

- Always keep your résumé up to date. Add new experiences and skill sets you develop. A good rule is to review your résumé at least once per year (such as in January). This allows you to update information and prepare for any potential job applications the following school year.

- Ensure your immunizations and any updates on fingerprints (most districts require) are complete. Place reminders on your calendar to ensure you reapply or update these items.

- Always keep your credential or license up to date and renew as needed.

- Keep your records and qualifications up to date to ensure you remain eligible and won't encounter any wrinkles or gaps in your ability to work in schools.

Create Your Sub Survival Kit

Empowered substitutes carry a sub survival kit to every assignment. Having such a kit is a proactive way to make sure you have everything you need for the day, as well as some fallback activities to supplement plans the regular teacher left, if necessary. We suggest having a physical survival kit, as well as some items you access digitally. For instance, keep your physical survival kit in a tote bag, a backpack, or even in a rolling cart—it's your choice! Here are some suggestions for the items to keep in your physical survival kit. We provide some ideas for a digital kit later in this chapter (see page 8).

- Teaching supplies:
    - Pens and pencils
    - Dry-erase markers
    - Highlighters
    - Notepad
    - Sticky notes
    - Stickers or stamps (the more fun, the better!)
    - Whistle (for playground duty)
- Personal care items:
    - Lunch and snacks
    - Refillable water bottle
    - Extra eyeglasses (if needed)
    - Tennis shoes (if your assignment includes supervising the playground, teaching physical education, or serving another campus duty that requires sure footing)
    - Small umbrella (in case you have bus duty when it's raining)
- Personalized business cards: Include your name, email address, cell phone number, and certifications. You can share them when checking in at the office or when introducing yourself to other teachers in the school.

Prepare Your Backup Plans

As a guest teacher, it's important you walk into a classroom with total confidence and, after completing the planned activities (and even if there are no plans, which is rare), you handle the remaining time using relevant activities to support student learning. To prepare, we recommend you compile or organize a variety of quick-grab or go-to activities you can use when you need to fill time with students. You might print some quick-grab activities or create a digital survival kit. For example, you might set up a Google folder to store various resources, creating subfolders for different grade ranges or categories, such as mathematics games or ideas for *brain breaks* (short, intentional breaks designed to help students recharge and refocus), you can access quickly online. Here are some specific suggestions for go-to activities when you need to fill some time while teaching or simply renew your students' interest or active participation when their attention is waning.

Read-Aloud Books

There are numerous websites, such as Goodreads (www.goodreads.com/list/tag/read-aloud) that suggest books you can read aloud. These books don't take a lot of time to read and are organized by grade bands. But don't assume you can only use read-alouds with elementary students—even students in middle or high school enjoy being read to. Carry a few age-appropriate books that could lead to interesting discussions during which students make connections to content they are learning or their past experiences. Some examples of good read-aloud books include the following.

- *Diary of a Fly* by Doreen Cronin
- *Dear Zoo* by Rod Campbell
- *Z Is for Moose!* by Kelly Bingham
- *Martin's Big Words: The Life of Dr. Martin Luther King Jr.* by Doreen Rappaport
- *Ramona the Pest* by Beverly Cleary
- *Ish* by Peter H. Reynolds

In addition to read-aloud books, consider keeping a book of funny poems handy that students would enjoy listening to. The classic poem collection is *Where the Sidewalk Ends* by Shel Silverstein. Other poetry books include the following.

- *The Complete Nonsense Book* by Edward Lear
- *Falling Up* by Shel Silverstein
- *I'm Just No Good at Rhyming* by Chris Harris
- *A Light in the Attic* by Shel Silverstein
- *Be Glad Your Nose Is on Your Face and Other Poems* by Jack Prelutsky
- *The Biggest Burp Ever: Funny Poems for Kids* by Kenn Nesbitt
- *Owl Moon* by Jane Yolen

One more book category to consider is the *How-to-Draw* book series, which can offer quick activities students of all ages enjoy.

- *How to Draw 101 Cute Stuff for Kids* by Sophia Elizabeth
- *How to Draw 101 Animals* by Dan Green

When selecting a book to read aloud, we suggest checking with a neighboring teacher at the school to ensure the book's appropriateness relative to the grade level and content. For example, a neighboring teacher in middle school could affirm whether a young adult fiction book is appropriate for students in a sixth-grade English class. In addition, be aware that some schools may have an approved list of books to use for read-alouds. By checking with a neighboring teacher or site administrator, you can get the necessary information. Avoid any books that might be controversial due to their content.

Easy-to-Implement Games

Chapter 4 (page 33) provides specific activities and ideas for engaging students; however, we suggest having some universally usable games ready to go. These games can incorporate any content and are applicable at multiple grade levels. They include the following.

- **Telephone:** Students whisper a message or statement from person to person. For example, the message could be a known phrase like, "The moon shines bright on a clear night," or one that uses vocabulary words or a literary device (such as alliteration) like, "The marvelous mouse moved mountains to munch the macadamias." Or start with a funny phrase like, "For Christmas this year, I will ask Santa for a purple dinosaur." Inevitably, the message changes along the way. When the last person says what message they heard aloud, it's often quite different from where it began. This game teaches students about the importance of listening closely. It is also an interesting jumping-off point to talk to older students (ages ten or eleven and up) about how information changes through different channels (like social media). To avoid inappropriate messages from making the rounds, we suggest providing the starter sentence (from a list, for example) rather than having students create their own.

- **Twenty questions:** This guessing game engages students in reasoning and logical thinking. Choose one student to be the "answerer" who knows *the answer*—a person, place, or thing the other students will try to guess. Students will have twenty opportunities to ask questions to find the answer. For example, students might start with a question like, "Is it smaller than a bowling ball?" and lead to the final question, "Is it a pencil sharpener?" You can adapt the topic to relate to the current content students are learning. For example, if students in grade 5 are learning about the American Revolution, the answer might be the Boston Tea Party, and students might first ask whether the answer is a person, place, or event.

- **Draw a picture:** Give students a blank piece of paper and ask them to draw something from memory or something that makes them happy and relaxed. This can lead to a positive social-emotional discussion about being aware of what makes people less stressed.

- **Silent ball:** You'll need one small ball for this activity, appropriately sized for the age of your students. Clear an area in the center of the room and select a leader to start. The leader counts down "3, 2, 1, silent" and passes the ball to another student. This student then passes the ball to another student. Students must sit down if they drop the ball, miss a pass, or make any noise. Whoever remains standing at the end is the winner. In addition to burning kinetic energy, this activity builds hand-eye coordination and nonverbal communication skills.

- **Would you rather?** In this activity, students are presented with two choices. They vote on the choice they prefer. For example, ask students, "Would you rather own a coffee shop or fast food restaurant?" For students in grades K–3, ask, "Would you rather have the ability to fly or be invisible?" Give students eight to ten opportunities to make choices. Students can respond by raising their hand, voting electronically (using a tool such as Kahoot; see https://kahoot.com), or moving to different sides of the room based on their answer. You can obtain a list of questions online, such as those on Parent Portfolio (see https://parentportfolio.com/would-you-rather-questions-for-kids). Tailor choices to the content students are learning. For example, if students are in a fractions unit, ask, "Would you rather have $5/12$ or $7/16$ of a pizza?"). In social studies, you could ask students, "Would you rather live in ancient Rome or ancient Egypt, or witness the Gettysburg Address or the signing of the Declaration of Independence?"

Worksheets at a Variety of Levels

Countless websites offer free worksheets for all students. Just search *worksheets* online, and you can easily find fun and appropriate worksheets for the grade level of students with whom you are working. Some substitutes elect to print several worksheets and carry them in their teaching bag to use to fill time with students as needed. Here are some printable worksheet websites.

- Education.com (www.education.com/worksheets)
- K5 Learning (www.k5learning.com/free-worksheets-for-kids)
- Super Teacher Worksheets (www.superteacherworksheets.com)

Make the Most of Your Resources

It's possible you already have resources at your fingertips. For example, do you have a friend or acquaintance in the teaching profession? Perhaps you know a former teacher willing to talk with you about how to make your experience as a substitute more successful or share helpful resources. These are examples of your most powerful resources. There are also a number of bloggers and vloggers offering suggestions for classroom management and instruction. Finally, you can find many resources on Pinterest (see https://pinterest.com) and other social media. Here are some websites that provide information on numerous topics and teaching strategies.

- Cult of Pedagogy (www.cultofpedagogy.com)
- Edutopia (www.edutopia.org)
- TeacherMade (www.freetech4teachers.com)
- TeachHUB (www.teachhub.com)
- TeachThought (www.teachthought.com)

There is no shortage of educational resources available through blogs and social media. We suggest you review a few and follow or bookmark the ones that best suit your needs. If you create a digital toolkit, you can bookmark those sites you find helpful to quickly access the information.

Get Ready for the Requests

Once you complete the application process and a district approves you as a substitute teacher, you will likely receive requests to substitute very quickly. Say you just received your first phone call asking you to serve as a substitute at a school—now what? Here, we'll walk through some tips to help you prepare for the assignment.

Learn About the Assignment

Knowing about the assignment before you get to the school will prepare and empower you. Successful subs have their questions ready to ask about the assignment so they can gather as much information as possible. You might even create a list of questions on your phone or in a special notebook, so they're always readily available, and record the answers to keep on hand. Here are some general questions to ask.

- "Is this a short-term assignment? How many days can I anticipate the assignment will last?"
- "What is the nature of the assignment (Grade level? Course? Specialized classroom or assignment?)?"
- "What substitute plans are available?"
- "Is there a specific parking spot I should use?"
- "Is it possible to speak to the teacher?"

It is likely you will receive a call for an assignment on a day you're unavailable or the assignment might not feel comfortable or like a good fit for you. Please know it's OK to share your concerns or questions about the assignment and ask for more information. We discuss some ideas later in this chapter for getting more information from the teacher.

Before deciding not to accept an assignment, it's important to remember two things. First, every assignment can be a growth or learning experience that builds your background and knowledge. Second, many districts monitor substitute activity, and if a person frequently declines assignments, the district may call the person less frequently or even remove the person from the call list.

Call the Teacher to Get Further Insights

Ideally, you will have access to the teacher to get more specifics about your sub assignment, particularly if the assignment lasts longer than one or two days. If you speak to the teacher, here are some questions you can ask.

- "What are your highest priorities for student learning when I'm there?"
- "Who are the student leaders I might call on for assistance?"
- "Are there any students who need specific monitoring (students with health issues or behavior issues, for example)?"
- "What special activities, if any, should I expect (such as assemblies or other special events)?"
- "What login information do I need to access the online tools you use daily? What are your tech policies for students (phones, non-school websites, and so on)?"
- "Where do you keep your sub plans, seating chart, and so on?"
- "What other duties do I need to fulfill during the day (for example, recess duty, pick-up or drop-off, and so on)?"
- "Are there multiple courses to teach each day? Are they all in the same classroom?" (For secondary students)
- "What information is important for me to know? Are there any paraprofessionals who work with the program?" (For specialty classes)

Figure 1.1 (page 14) provides a template to record information based on the questions you will ask the office staff, and if available, the teacher you are subbing for. Use this form for note-taking whenever you receive an assignment.

Substitute Assignment Notes	
Site and grade level: Dates of assignment:	Principal: Secretary: Other support person:
Teacher name: Substitute plans available? Y / N Is there a specific parking spot I should use? Y / N Space number: Can I contact the teacher? Y / N Phone or email:	
<ul><li>What are your highest priorities for student learning when I'm there?</li><li>Who are the student leaders I might call on for assistance?</li><li>Are there any students who need specific monitoring (students with health issues or behavior issues, for example)?</li><li>What special activities, if any, should I expect (such as assemblies or other special events)?</li><li>What login information do I need to access the online tools you use daily? What are your tech policies for students (phones, non-school websites, and so on)?</li><li>Where do you keep your sub plans, seating chart, and so on?</li><li>What other duties do I need to fulfill during the day (for example, recess duty, pick-up or drop-off, and so on)?</li><li>Are there multiple courses to teach each day? Are they all in the same classroom? (For secondary students)</li><li>What information is important for me to know? Are there any paraprofessionals who work with the program? (For specialty classes)</li></ul>	

Figure 1.1: Assignment notes template.

*Visit **go.SolutionTree.com/teacherefficacy** to download a free reproducible version of this figure.*

Plan Your Preparation

Now that you know the assignment and have gathered information, here's a quick to-do list before showing up to the job.

- Confirm the time you should arrive.
- Make sure you know the school's location and map out how much time it will take you to get there—and plan to arrive early!
- Choose items for your toolkit (what you bring or have available digitally) based on your assignment.

We've have created a Google Form (see https://google.com/forms/about) of figure 1.1, which you can access digitally on your phone or computer using the following QR code or visiting: https://tinyurl.com/ym2aj7up. You can also save a copy of the form in your personal drive to use each time you need to gather information about a new assignment. By completing the form for each assignment, you'll have an organized record of all your assignments.

Speaking From Experience...
Advice From Practicing or Former Subs

"Always have some extra pencils for students who have forgotten or lost them to avoid unnecessary trips to the locker or cubby."

"Never underestimate the value of comfortable shoes!"

"Pack an easy-to-grab snack!"

This chapter's focus is on getting organized and prepared for a successful substitute teaching experience. Use the reproducible "My Notes and Reflection" (page 16) to record your thoughts about this chapter. Chapter 2 (page 17) discusses some strategies you can use to start your day as a substitute teacher with confidence and professionalism.

My Notes and Reflection: Prepare for Success

1. What is one new consideration I learned after reading this chapter?

2. What do I have left on my to-do list to get ready to serve as a substitute?

3. What items do I want to ensure I have in my survival kit?

4. How might I organize my backup activities to access them quickly when needed?

5. Who might I contact as a resource for ideas as I prepare to work in schools?

6. What additional questions do I want to ask before any assignment so I can prepare?

CHAPTER 2

Start Out Strong

As a substitute teacher, you must see yourself as part of a team of professionals. You are, in essence, a guest teacher who is supporting an absent teacher. From the moment you arrive in the parking lot to the time you leave at the end of the day, you are visible and make an impression on students, parents, and other team members at the school. This chapter provides recommendations for working at a school in a manner that builds connections and proactively sets the stage for positive, professional, and supportive interactions with site leaders, school staff, fellow teachers, and any parents who happen to be at the school.

> **Key Points**
> - Substitute teachers must demonstrate the same professionalism as other teachers. Consider yourself a *guest teacher*.
> - Your experience at a school will be more successful when you connect with leaders, the office staff, and other teachers.
> - By getting to school early, you'll have the chance to proactively prepare and organize.

Dress Professionally

While some schools have more casual dress expectations for their staff, it's always better to err on the side of being more formal than less formal. A good rule is to adhere to business-like attire. That said, you can still express your personality in your clothing choices, like with bold colors or a funny tie. In general, avoid jeans and clothing others might not consider professional (that is, anything others might perceive as revealing or inappropriate). If you're unsure of the expectations, you can ask the office staff or other teachers when you first learn about your assignment. For example, if as part of your assignment you have recess duty or need to sit on the floor while teaching students, it will be important to wear comfortable shoes and avoid restrictive clothing. If your assignment is to teach physical education, it may be appropriate to wear athletic clothing.

Arrive Early

As a general rule, plan to arrive *at least* thirty minutes to an hour before instruction starts. There are two reasons you'll want to arrive early for your assignment. First, arriving early ensures you have plenty of time to connect with the front office staff and orient yourself to the classroom (we describe this orientation in the following sections, beginning on page 19). It also gives you time to access lesson plans and course materials. Arriving early allows you to walk through your plan for the day. Second, by arriving early, you avoid any traffic jams that often happen when parents drop off their child before school.

Check In With the Office

The office staff members, which typically include the school secretary and clerks, are your lifeline to everything at the school. The office staff are the hub for all the activities taking place at the school and know the right people to call when needed. It's possible you will need to show a photo ID when first arriving at the school, so be sure to bring one with you. When you check in, the office staff or one of the site administrators will let you know where to locate your room and sub plans. Office staff may also provide the following when you check in.

- Room keys
- Name badge
- Login information for accessing technology tools in the classroom
- Location of teacher's sub plans (if you don't receive this information in advance)
- Attendance and lunch count procedures (if applicable; many schools use an electronic system to take attendance and submit lunch counts)
- Information about any special events or activities you should know about (such as assemblies, fire drills, special visitors, and so on, if you don't already have this information)
- Location of staff breakroom and restrooms (Be sure to ask if you need a key for the restrooms!)

Make sure the office staff have your cell phone number (accomplish this quickly with business cards) and confirm the best communication method if a need arises in the classroom, such as a student injury or other need requiring immediate support. Most likely, office staff will direct you to call the office in such a circumstance, since staff can usually instantly connect and communicate with site administrators and campus supervisors using walkie-talkies.

Before heading to the classroom, confirm any details you need about the assignment and the processes for checking out at the end of the day.

Connect With Your Teaching Neighbors

If possible, stop in the classrooms next to your assigned room and introduce yourself. The other teachers nearby will likely be familiar with the routine in the absent teacher's classroom and may be able to answer any questions you might have throughout the day. It's also helpful to exchange cell phone numbers in case you need to ask a quick question during the day, such as to confirm a school routine or expectation. It's also likely neighboring teachers have insights about specific students and suggestions for addressing any specific behavior concerns. Finally, the neighboring teachers might have some resources they can share, such as an appropriate read-aloud book or other activity.

Check Out the Room

Once you get inside the classroom, get a quick lay of the land. First, locate your sub plans—they will likely provide you with insight into the day's schedule and expectations for your teaching. Second, locate the seating chart (or charts) or, if the school uses an online attendance system, log in to access the system. Finally, locate the materials you'll need to access for the first major activity or lesson segment. Try to mentally walk through the rest of the day's schedule so you can anticipate transitions or other preparation needs.

Take a Breath and Get Ready to Greet Your Students

By arriving well before students arrive at the school, you have time to not only prepare the materials you'll be using but also yourself mentally for the day. Some teachers call it *getting their game face on*—in other words, telling yourself you're going to have a successful day and adopting the attitude of a capable and successful teacher. Chapter 3 (page 23) builds on the strategies for starting on a great note by examining ways to fulfill that picture of success by building strong connections with your students.

Don't Be Afraid to Ask for Help

Nobody expects you to have all the answers, especially when you're in a new assignment as a substitute teacher. It's always better to ask a question to get the correct information rather than guessing at an answer and hoping you're correct.

If you find yourself with a question as you're actively teaching, jot it down. When there's a break between classes or during recess or lunch, find one of the neighboring teachers or a site administrator who can answer your question. Or, if you have a neighboring teacher's cell phone number, you can always text your question. Sometimes, the absent teacher you are filling in for is still available on site and provided a cell phone number just in case; however, if the regular teacher does not provide the number, it is best to leave notes for the teacher.

Don't Shy Away From Opportunities to Learn

You may be subbing on a day when there are opportunities to get some professional learning. For instance, you may be subbing on a day when all the teachers in the grade level or course meet as a collaborative team during their planning period. There may be an afternoon professional development activity with a focus on a new instructional practice. Rather than skipping these opportunities, ask if you can sit in on the meeting. In most cases, teachers welcome the opportunity to include others. By participating, you'll get to know other members of the school staff, including some teachers for whom you might be subbing in the future. Also, it is an opportunity to gain insight into what the students are learning and strategies for teaching and assessing specific skills. Think of each new experience as an opportunity to learn and build relationships.

We hope as you read this chapter, you began to feel more empowered to walk into a substitute teaching setting. By checking in with the school staff and making connections from the beginning, you'll already establish a system of support and start positive relationships in the school. Use the reproducible "My Notes and Reflection" to record your thoughts about this chapter. Chapter 3 (page 23) focuses on your connections with students.

Speaking From Experience . . .
Advice From Practicing or Former Subs

"Introduce yourself to the teacher in the classroom next door so you have someone to ask questions about school policies and so on."

"Be neat and dress professionally."

"Build positive relationships with the office staff."

My Notes and Reflection: Start Out Strong

1. What are my takeaways from this chapter?

2. When I consider potential sub assignments, which would I find most challenging? Least challenging?

3. What is my mindset when it comes to taking on a challenging assignment?

4. What additional questions do I want to ask the classroom teacher or office staff members before I start the day?

5. What questions might I ask my teacher friends to gain more insight about starting the day strong?

CHAPTER 3

Connect With Students

From the time students enter the classroom until they leave for the day, how they connect with others can impact their mindset and learning. Of course, these connections include both interactions with their teachers and substitute teachers when their teachers are absent. In school, relationships are key, and as a substitute, you need some strategies to connect with students and build a foundation for your relationships with them.

> **Key Points**
> - Use strategies to build familiarity and rapport with students.
> - Use appropriate humor and incorporate a little fun to ease tensions when working with a new class of students.
> - Give students brain breaks to split up a long class session, learn something about your students, and engage in a fun activity or conversation.

Establishing connections builds trust with students, and it takes time. As a substitute teacher, you may not have that luxury. Yet research shows when students feel trust and connections with teachers (even substitutes), they contribute to a positive learning environment, and students are more likely to actively participate and interact with you (Hattie, 2023; Poulou, 2017). This chapter provides some considerations to help you connect with students and have a positive impact during the time you spend with them. These basic strategies and reminders will help you build a meaningful and engaging rapport with students and help you connect and relate to them.

Be Vulnerable, but Not a Pushover

When you're first serving as a substitute teacher, it's natural to feel anxious and worry about how you'll connect with students. For example, you may be serving in a high school classroom for the first time, or in a kindergarten classroom when most of your experience is with older students. It's OK for you to let students know this is a new context for you and you expect their assistance, but your goal is to bridge the gap until their teacher returns. To build rapport and trust, be open about your mistakes—you can even ask for help if needed. Students will see you as honest and transparent. However, as some of our favorite subs share, "Never let them see you sweat." In other words, present yourself as a capable guest teacher, one who may not know everything about the classroom content, but someone who has good judgement, can make decisions, and is in charge despite not being the regular teacher.

Build Rapport and Trust

There is a strong link between teachers' connections with students and student success in learning, and research supports that, when teachers establish positive relationships with students, classroom behavior improves and disruptive behavior decreases (Cook et al., 2018). So, what does it mean to connect with students? It means helping students feel that others value them, having empathy, building trust, and demonstrating respect. As a substitute teacher, it's important to remember some students may be sensitive about their teacher being absent, especially if the teacher is out due to illness. They may be worried or feel threatened that you're there instead of their teacher. Some students may feel uneasy because the routine is different. It's not personal. There is plenty of brain research that discusses how a new or challenging situation can cause students to feel threatened, resulting in strong emotions, which can hijack or override their ability to learn (Hammond, 2015). So it's important to establish a positive relationship with all students. Every teacher has the goal of establishing a safe and engaging classroom climate. As a substitute teacher, you can support that goal by using strategies to connect with students and establishing good working relationships. Here are some proven strategies for building rapport and trust with students.

Meet and Greet

One of the most important moments of the day is when you purposefully greet students as they enter your classroom. Your greeting sets the tone for the rest of the interactions you'll have that day, so it's important to welcome students to the class. Their first interaction with you will tell them who you are as a person and how you regard them as students. A good practice (until you know student names) is to call students *friends* or *scholars* (but check in with the regular classroom teacher or a neighboring teacher on site to see if there's a preferred term).

Let your greetings be natural and age appropriate. The absent teacher may have some traditions as students enter the room (for instance, some teachers keep a chart outside their door with choices for how students each want the teacher to greet them, such as with a fist bump, a high five, and so on). If you know and are comfortable with these greetings, feel free to continue them throughout your time in the classroom. Approach your greeting in a way that reflects your personality and is age-appropriate for the students. Here are some suggestions.

- "Good morning! I'm [Name], your guest teacher today. What's your name? Nice to meet you."
- "Hi! What's your name? I'm [Name]. I'm glad you're here today!"

Be aware, however, that middle or high school students can sniff out inauthentic attempts to connect. They might consider the previous list of greetings as you trying to "butter them up." Instead, you can simply say, "I hope you're having a good day," "Good to see you," or "I'm glad you're here."

Let Them Get to Know You

A fun way for students to connect with you in your role as a substitute teacher is to engage them in a short question-and-answer session (lasting five to ten minutes) during which they can ask questions about you: where you went to school, where you grew up, and so on. Perhaps you have a special musical talent or had an unusual job. You can give them the topic, and they ask fifteen questions to narrow down the answer. Think about what personal experiences you have that others might find interesting. Are you a superfan of an athletic team or band, or a movie series fanatic (think *Star Wars* or *Harry Potter*)? Are you learning a new skill? Perhaps there's a funny story you can share about your struggle to learn. Do you speak another language? Use your uniqueness to your advantage. It may be your superpower! Again, always be aware of the age group and the appropriateness of the information you share.

Use Appropriate Humor

Many successful substitutes share they use humor to connect with students. This doesn't necessarily mean they tell jokes, but they bring humor into their conversations with students. Using humor can result in a more engaging classroom and help ease any tension that might come with a new person taking over for the regular teacher. Humor can be silly or self-deprecating, but it should *never* focus on putting down or being sarcastic toward others. Err on the side of silly versus sophisticated. For example, there are several online sources for dad jokes you can share to get a quick laugh from your class. However, before using any joke, use your professional filters: be sure your humor is acceptable for the grade level of the class and will pass the *appropriateness test*. (To determine this, ask yourself, "Will I get a phone call about this?").

Make a Connection to the Learning by Sharing Your Experiences

Students love stories. Find ways to connect your experiences to what students are learning using stories. If you're helping students work on essays, for example, you can share some tips about how you improved your writing ability when you were in high school. Perhaps you had a special formula. Maybe there's a mathematical trick you can demonstrate that was helpful for you as a student. For example, your favorite mathematics teacher shared with you how to check whether a number is a multiple of 9: if the sum of the digits in a number is a multiple of 9, then the number itself is a multiple of 9. As an example, if you take the number 234 and add the digits 2 + 3 + 4, they total 9. Therefore, 234 is a multiple of 9.

Acknowledge Each Student

Students will more likely connect and engage with what is happening in a classroom when teachers show they care and have personal regard for students. As a substitute teacher, your first opportunity to show this regard is when you're taking attendance. If you're unsure how to pronounce a name, ask the student and let the student know it's important to you to pronounce the name correctly. You might ask students each the name they prefer you call them. For example, a student named Isabella may prefer you call her Izzy. You could also acknowledge each student during roll call by asking a quick question, such as, "Do you have a sibling at this school?" or "How many years have you been at this school?"

Another strategy to acknowledge each student is using a random process, such as picking sticks or randomly selecting students from a seating chart to respond to questions or lead a group. This way, you'll be engaging all students over the course of the lesson (rather than only engaging the students who have their hands raised).

Be Present in the Work

Avoid simply sitting at the teacher's desk while students are working—let the teacher's desk collect dust! As a substitute teacher, it's important to circulate and be present in the activities students are completing, even if you expect students to work independently. Actively move around the room, asking students how it's going and showing interest in what they're doing. Offer assistance when needed. When students see you actively engaging in what they're doing, they'll be more likely to engage and focus on the activity.

Use Engaging Transitions and Routines

During the instructional day, students must make transitions. Transitions may involve physical movement to and from other parts of the school or simply changing focus from one activity to the next. Successful transitions are efficient and accomplish the task of getting students to engage in the next activity without losing instructional time. Here we recommend a process for implementing effective transitions.

1. Plan each transition intentionally, including what you want students to do before the transition, the signal you will use to gain their attention, and the method for moving on to the next activity. (Note: There are numerous ways to gain students' attention with a quick signal, such as a callback or a raised hand to get everyone to pause talking. We provide additional ideas in chapter 4, page 33.).

2. Prepare students by getting their attention and sharing how they will transition. For example, you might say, "In five minutes, we will be going to recess. When I give the signal, I want you to line up by table groups. I will know your table is ready to line up when all materials are put away and chairs are pushed in. I will call your table group when I see your table is ready."

3. Use your signal to start the transition.

4. Monitor and redirect individual students as needed.

You can use class lineups not only to transition in and out of the classroom but also to randomly assign students to groups. For example, you can ask students to line up by their birthday month, and then divide the line into smaller groups. This process mixes up students for smaller conversations. Here are some ways you could ask students to line up.

- By salsa spice level (line up by how spicy you like your salsa)
- By color (everyone wearing a blue shirt, for example)
- By birthday month (January is first in line, then February, and so on)

You can also use music to signal changes. Create a playlist of popular songs (use the "clean" versions!) and play a little music when you want students to transition to the next activity. When the music ends, students should be in place. The key to transitions is to go beyond just telling students to line up or move to the next activity by incorporating a little novelty or fun.

Incorporate Brain Breaks

Sometimes students need a break from working, so consider using brain breaks. *Brain breaks* are quick, structured breaks that give students an opportunity to move around, re-center themselves, or simply refresh their thinking by taking a break. In fact, research demonstrates a strong connection between having short physical and mindfulness breaks and increased student attention and academic success (Müller et al., 2021). You can structure brain breaks as a whole-class activity or allow students to choose how they take a break. Some examples of how you could incorporate a five- to ten-minute brain break include the following.

- Guided stretch or movement activity
- Fun brainteasers
- Partner games like rock, paper, scissors or thumb wars
- Whole-group activities such as Would you rather?

Create a Collaborative Atmosphere

Rather than sitting and getting information from you, students appreciate opportunities to work collaboratively with other students. According to the Center for Teaching Innovation (2023), students benefit greatly when they work together in pairs or small groups. When students work together, they actively engage instead of passively listen. By letting go of total control (or by not being the *sage on the stage*), you honor students' past learning and trust them to be problem solvers with their peers. In chapter 4 (page 33), we suggest structures for collaborative interactions among students. You can also build in a structure so student teams report out their solutions and share any new learnings they experience.

Speaking From Experience . . .
Advice From Practicing or Former Subs

"Talk to students before class, in the halls, or around the school."

"Remember, you are not the students' friend; you are their teacher."

"Model politeness."

"Find a trustworthy student to help locate or explain certain procedures."

"Walk around the room. Never sit at the desk, especially during a test."

Demonstrate an Inclusive and Respectful Mindset

Students come to school with different cultural backgrounds, economic realities, and learning experiences. Some students may be learning to become bilingual. Others may have unique learning needs. However, regardless of any differences among students, it's important to welcome and include *all* students. Use an inclusive teaching mindset in which you intentionally engage all students in meaningful, relevant, and accessible ways. This means as a teacher, you are responsive to students' needs and respectful of their differences. To that end, avoid using labels. You may hear others reference some students as their "low kids" or "my ELs" when describing a group. This is not a respectful practice. Students are not their ethnicity, their language, nor their diagnoses.

> ### How Would You Respond?
>
> Your class has worked independently on their assigned tasks for thirty minutes. You have noticed more students getting off task and losing momentum. How might you refocus or re-energize the class?
>
> **Possible Strategies**
> - Make sure you circulate, are available to answer questions, and monitor what's happening.
> - Have students share out the skills in which they feel confident and any they find more challenging. Perhaps one student or a team of students can enlighten others in the class.
> - Take a quick five-minute stretch or brain break. Use music to cue students into the break and then again when break time is up. Students can move around the classroom but must return to their seats when you give the signal.

Acknowledge the Regular Teacher's Absence

The district may assign you to substitute in a classroom where the teacher is on long-term leave due to serious illness or circumstances. Depending on the situation, it may be appropriate to take time to have the class compose a note or draw a special picture with a message to the regular teacher. Another idea is to have the class take a selfie or quick video to send get-well wishes. Before doing anything, however, we suggest you check with school administrators to make sure such an action is appropriate.

A substitute teacher has the opportunity to impact students not only academically but also socially and emotionally. By establishing yourself as a capable, credible *guest* teacher and demonstrating you care about the students, you set the tone for building positive relationships and much more satisfying experiences.

Use the reproducible "My Notes and Reflection" to record your thoughts about this chapter. Chapter 4 (page 33) will dig into the key practices and structures to help you manage all that happens in the classroom.

My Notes and Reflection: Connect With Students

1. What key points do I want to prioritize from this chapter?

2. What might students find interesting in my background that would provide a connection? What's my superpower?

3. What strategy might I use to incorporate brain breaks into the day?

4. What transitions will students likely be making during the day? How might I get information about transitions?

5. When I think about a teacher in my own life who established trust and respect, what did that look like? What might I do initially with students to establish trust and respect?

CHAPTER 4

Make It Manageable and Engaging

Thinking about substitute teaching may take you back to when you were in school. Do you remember how you felt when a substitute teacher walked into your classroom? Can you remember some great ones? Do you remember students in your class who smirked when they saw the substitute and spent the day being uncooperative? Did you feel sorry for a substitute and even try to help? Now you are the substitute! With some good classroom-management skills and basic knowledge of how classroom structures work (including those we highlight in this chapter), you will be a positive substitute-teacher memory in the minds of your students.

> **Key Points**
> - All classrooms benefit from having clear expectations and routines. As a substitute, you follow through with established expectations and routines. If they don't exist, you may need to establish some general expectations.
> - By using different ways to structure your instruction, you'll increase the likelihood of engaging students.

Be a Successful Classroom Manager

Before you can be a successful teacher, you must be a successful manager of students. This means students know you are the boss, and you know you are the boss. It also means students are truly clear about what behaviors you expect of them, which means you must be clear about how you want students to behave. This clarity will help you set up students for success, whether you have them for a fifty-minute class or six hours. Starting class explaining your student behavior expectations and then using positive reinforcement is the recipe for a great substitute day!

The very sight of a substitute teacher at the front of the classroom can stir a lot of different emotions for students, including feelings of unease, stress, anxiety, worry, panic, sadness, and also the excitement of the unknown. For some students, it can also mean a "free day" from rules and work. As a substitute teacher, just being aware students have these emotions, feelings, and thoughts is a good starting place. Putting students at ease with warmth and a nice welcome goes a long way. After that, the best way to help worrying students, as well as those who think it might be a free day, is to establish you are a guest teacher here to run the class well, and you have high expectations for good behavior and hard work.

Hopefully, the classroom teacher left you information on the established classroom-management procedures, such as putting students' names on the board to show who exhibits positive or negative behaviors, passing out "good" tickets, and asking you (as the guest teacher) to leave a note at the end of the day that includes information about students' behavior. Usually, a teacher who has a good management system in place leaves strong details for you to follow, and usually, the students know the routines and expectations. Luckily, this is—or should be—the reality of most of your experiences. You can get to know the established system and fit right into it. In addition, there are always students in each class willing to help explain the system to you. You can ask students to raise their hands and volunteer to answer some of the following questions.

- "What are your classroom rules?"
- "What do you and the class receive if you follow the rules?"
- "What happens if someone doesn't follow the rules?"

The more challenging issue is when you walk into a room where those routines and expectations are unclear to students, even when their regular teacher is present. This is a time for you to establish your own expectations, rewards, and consequences. Stay positive and be proactive. You are the adult in charge of the room. Stay calm and set rules and expectations.

Here are some elementary classroom rules you could use.

- Stay seated and raise your hand if you need permission to leave your seat.
- Raise your hand to talk or share.
- Use a quiet or inside voice at all times.
- Ask for help if needed.

- Follow directions.
- Be kind.
- Be respectful.
- Ask two classmates for clarification or help before asking the teacher.

And here are some sample rules for secondary classrooms.

- Stay seated.
- Follow directions.
- Show respect to other students and the teacher.
- Do not use unapproved electronic devices.
- Do not use unapproved internet sites on devices.
- Make good decisions.
- Be respectful.

Once you go over the rules for the day, take a moment to remind students of the rewards and consequences attached to those rules.

Possible Rewards

It is wise to check with a neighboring teacher to see whether there are any schoolwide guidelines regarding appropriate versus inappropriate rewards. For example, some schools may have decided that free time or "no homework" passes are inappropriate rewards for good student behavior. The more information you have about a school and its management systems, the easier it is for you to easily fit in and better support students.

In elementary classrooms, you could use the following rewards.

- Students love positive feedback! Praise! Praise! Praise!
- Students earn a job as a classroom helper.
- Students earn first in line for recess or lunch.
- Students get their name on the board with a star next to it.
- Students earn stickers.
- Students earn a special pencil (a good addition to your substitute survival kit).
- Students earn free time.
- Students earn art or game time at the end of the day.

- Students complete the reproducible "I Did Awesome Today!" (page 48). Send this form home with the student. Make a copy to leave for the regular classroom teacher. Younger students can draw pictures instead of writing a narrative.
- Students receive a Super Star award (see page 49 for a reproducible version) they can take home or leave for the regular teacher.

In secondary classrooms, use the following rewards.

- Students earn some free time to draw or work on something they enjoy. Some of the elementary rewards work for older students, who also love "hang out" time with their classmates if appropriate.
- Students earn extra homework time.
- Students can work in pairs or with a friend.
- Students complete the reproducible "I Did Awesome Today!" (page 48). Send the completed form home with the student and make a copy to leave for the regular classroom teacher.

Full-Class Reward

The full-class reward strategy tells the students every time you find them following the rules and doing their work; you will write a letter on the board until the letters spell something like *recess* or *free time*. Once the word is completely spelled out, the class has earned extra recess time or free time in the classroom. Using positive reinforcement is always preferred over using negative consequences.

Table or Team Reward

Another very motivating way to reward students for following the rules is to reward groups of students. In the morning or at the beginning of the period, divide the class into teams if students aren't already sitting in natural teams (like at tables). Number the teams and write a vertical list on the board: *Team 1, Team 2, Team 3*, and so on. Every time a team is following directions and those students are doing what you want them to do, give the team a tally mark. At the end of the day or period, reward students using your discretion. You may decide to only reward the team with the most points, or you could reward the top three teams. It is up to you to determine how engaged the students are in the reward system. The reward can be free time at the end of the day or period, or leaving the classroom first at the end of class. For elementary school students, stickers are a huge motivator. All students usually like to know you will be reporting their good behavior back to their regular classroom teacher.

Management by Movement

One of the essential components of good classroom management is to continually walk around the classroom. Don't sit at the teacher's desk or in the front of the room. Instead, frequently walk around the room and between students' desks. By simply being on the move and watching what is going on in the classroom, you will decrease the number of negative student behaviors. *Management by movement* also projects confidence that you are in control of the classroom, and that confidence goes a long way in creating a successful day!

Get Students' Attention

One of the critical skills of any guest teacher is the ability to get students' attention 100 percent of the time. You may need to practice this with each class so students are aware of what cue you will use to gain their attention, and that you have high expectations they will follow the system you use.

A fun way to get students' attention is to use amusing callbacks. A *callback* is when you initiate the attention-getting signal by saying the first part of a phrase, and students complete the phrase. For example, you might say, "Class-class," and students respond, "Yes-yes!" Some classes already use callbacks, and you can check in with a trusted student to learn the ones the class already uses. If not, you can teach the class one or two. Be sure to consider the students' age group, although adults like using callbacks too, so your high school students may surprise you with enthusiasm for this strategy.

Following are some possible callback structures.

1. All set—You bet!
2. Are you ready?—We're ready!
3. Ready to rock?—Ready to roll!
4. Class, class—Yes, yes!
5. Hakuna—Matata!
6. To infinity—And beyond!
7. One, two, three, eyes on me—One, two, eyes on you!
8. Holy moly—Guacamole!
9. Waterfall—Shhhhh.
10. Chicka chicka—Boom boom!

Some classrooms have routines involving clapping to get attention. For example, the teacher might start the clap using a pattern commonly used to knock on a door (Clap-clap-a-clap-clap), and students respond with the answer (clap-clap). Another clapping variation involves students responding to your voice cues: "If you can hear my voice, clap once; if you can hear my voice, clap twice; if you can hear my voice, clap three times." Decide which routine you are most comfortable with and learn to use it with different classes. You can always change up the routine to keep things fresh for you. Use one clap routine one day, change it around, and use another clap routine when you have a different assignment. The important thing is to use the same clap routine or callback with the same group of students so they understand when to give you their full attention (that is, when you ask for it).

Address Students Who Don't Meet Your Behavior Expectations

There will be times when students don't meet your expectations for behavior and respect. Having consequences for these students is important and sends a message to the other students that you are serious about their behavior. Again, ask neighboring teachers or an administrator if there are appropriate agreed-on schoolwide consequences or any the school may not want to use. For example, many schools don't take away recess from students because it is important for students to have time for physical movement. Other schools may have a time-out area to send students to at recess. Ask around and learn as much as you can about how the school gives consequences.

Possible consequences include the following.

- Start with a warning and remind students of the rules and behavior expectations.

- Remove students from current seating arrangements if this is a possible cause of misbehavior.

- Give students a brief time-out (no talking or getting up) at their desks or at a location near you. For most students, a five-minute time-out is sufficient to redirect their behavior. You may occasionally have a student who will benefit from a longer time-out of ten to fifteen minutes. Remember, the younger the student, the shorter the time-out time should be because younger students have shorter attention spans.

- For elementary students, take away a portion of recess (that way, you can also get to the restroom and take a break). Many schools are moving away from taking recess away since students need to move and burn off their energy. This consequence is a compromise. You can keep the student inside for the first few minutes of recess and use the time to talk about and redirect the student's behavior so the student can get back on track. After your pep talk, let the student head out to recess, and you can enjoy your break as well.

- For upper-elementary and secondary students, isolate the student in a portion of the room and talk with the student about the behavior issues. Have the student complete the reproducible "Oops, I Didn't Make a Good Decision Today" (page 50). Send the completed form home with the student for the parents and report to the regular teacher on the end-of-day form. Make a copy of the completed form and leave it for the classroom teacher if possible.
- As a last resort, send the student to the office or a neighboring teacher's classroom (a teacher you have already talked with). Some schools already have buddy teachers in place. Buddy teachers will introduce themselves to you and let you know they are there to help. Other schools will not have buddy teachers, but you can always ask a neighboring teacher the protocols if you need to send a student out of the classroom. Many schools have counselors who can help de-escalate student situations. Asking a neighboring teacher about counselor support is also a good idea so you know all your options.

This is important to know: you cannot send a student into a hallway without supervision, have a student sit in the corner, or miss lunch or a snack. The goal is to discipline the student while respectfully teaching and correcting the behavior. No matter what happens with a student, it is always important to recognize you are the adult and a role model for younger people learning how to handle their emotions and impulses. This means *at no time* can you be disrespectful to students. This includes no yelling or belittling students, and no use of sarcasm or put-downs.

We cannot understate the importance of keeping calm and levelheaded—even when you face difficult situations. (We also discuss this in chapter 5, page 51.) You should have strategies for calming yourself down, such as deep breathing, counting to ten, taking a brief cool-off time-out, or taking a long drink of water. Find out what you can do to calm yourself if a student is pushing your buttons. If a student is dangerous or threatening in any way, you must take immediate action to get assistance. Call the front office immediately and send another student to the classroom next door for assistance. There is never an acceptable use for violence or threats from a student. Take action to remove the student from the classroom as soon as possible, then go back to your calming techniques and get on with your day.

Establish Instructional Structures

Your success as a substitute teacher directly relates to the structures and strategies you set up first thing in the morning or at the beginning of each class period. There are many different structures you can use, as well as hundreds of instructional strategies at your disposal. Learning about these structures and strategies will not only make your life easier but also keep students engaged and learning throughout the day or class period.

Whether working in a preschool, elementary school, middle school, or high school classroom, here are some of the multiple ways you can organize your teaching, student interactions, and learning.

Full-Class Instruction

Full-class instruction is when you talk and students listen. Use full-class instruction to go over the day's plans or the period's work instructions the regular teacher left for you. Make sure to compliment the students as they listen to you and be clear when delivering information. The idea is to gradually release the responsibility of getting work done to the students. To do this, begin with a full-class explanation or minilesson of the next lesson and activity. The better you get at clearly explaining lessons, concepts, and students' responsibilities, the smoother your day will go. In the book *Better Learning Through Structured Teaching: A Framework for the Gradual Release of Responsibility*, San Diego State University professors and coauthors Douglas Fisher and Nancy Frey (2014) describe the steps of this gradual release using the following sequence.

1. **Focused instruction:** *I do it*—This is when you (the teacher) are teaching the lesson, concept, or activity to the students, usually in a whole-group setting.

2. **Guided instruction:** *We do it*—Now you model the lesson, give examples, and answer any questions. You can work with a small group of students during the collaborative learning phase and help them get on task and assist in any way.

3. **Collaborative learning:** *You do it together*—You could have students work together in small groups to start the lesson or activity. (Read more about this process on page 41.)

4. **Independent learning:** *You do it alone*—Now you ask students each to complete the assignment on their own. (Read more about independent learning time on page 43.)

You can change and maneuver this sequence of the gradual release to meet the needs of your class at any specific time. For example, maybe students understand the lesson and don't need any guided instruction. Or maybe students have been overly chatty, and you want to skip the collaborative learning piece and jump right to independent learning. That is your decision as the guest teacher!

When doing full-class focused instruction, use a whiteboard to write some keywords or phrases about the lesson so there is a visual representation of what you are sharing. Make sure to have a way to get students' attention, so if they begin to talk among themselves, you know how to get them quiet again so you can continue your lesson. (See the suggestions on how to get your students' attention on page 37.) Use full-class instruction whenever you have a new concept or lesson to teach or need to give all students the same directions or information.

Cooperative Groups

Cooperative groups are a great strategy for having students work together in groups of three or four to complete a task. Best-selling author and researcher Robert J. Marzano (2001) identifies *cooperative learning* as a top teaching and learning strategy; his research shows students learn better when working and learning in peer groups. In *Classroom Instruction That Works*, Marzano, along with coauthors Debra J. Pickering and Jane E. Pollock (2001) share, "Of all classroom grouping strategies, cooperative learning may be the most flexible and powerful" (p. 91). Getting students to work together helps them achieve better results (Killian, 2015). The use of cooperative learning groups adds value to whole-class instruction and individual work.

Students are naturally social and enjoy talking to one another. Ensure your directions are clear for what students should be working on and the completed work products you expect at the end of the session. As groups get to work, walk around the room monitoring the groups and helping struggling groups and students get started or stay on task.

One effective way to organize the groups is to give each group member a job or role. For example, you can ask the members of the group to decide who will be the following.

- **Leader:** The person who keeps the group moving and on task
- **Scribe:** The person who takes notes on the discussion
- **Presenter:** The person who will present the group's findings to the class
- **Manager:** The person who watches the time and ensures everyone is participating and listening to all opinions and thoughts

You can use cooperative groups whenever you feel you are working with students who can concentrate on the task (and not be overly stimulated or distracted due to working with other students). An example of an activity to use with cooperative groups for grades 2–12 students involves reading an article. Provide the group with an interesting, age-appropriate article and have group members read it while underlining the especially interesting parts. Then have the group write a quick summary of the article, noting if group members agreed or disagreed with the article, to share with the class during share time. Carry some copies of interesting articles with you so if a lesson plan needs some additional activities, you can pull an article out of your bag and have students read and discuss it. You can find interesting free articles online at sites like ReadWorks (https://readworks.org).

Center Rotations in Small Groups

This structure takes preplanning but is very enjoyable for students. You create four or five centers with specific activities for students to participate in and learn from. Groups of students then move from center to center when you tell them it is time to move. Many teachers turn the lights off and on as a cue to move to the next center, or you can use a bell or other sound. Some elementary school examples of centers include the following.

- **Literacy centers:** In these centers, students can listen with headphones to a book being read out loud, do a daily written journal activity, read a book of their choice in a library section of the classroom, complete a grammar worksheet, or practice important vocabulary by sorting words into groups or writing words to practice spelling.

- **Mathematics centers:** A manipulatives center is where students use blocks and cubes to practice putting numbers together and counting; a numeracy center is where students complete a worksheet practicing their number facts; and a technology center is where students practice their mathematics on specific programs.

- **Free-time centers:** Create these centers when you have completed the regular teacher's lesson plans and still have time left in the period or day. You can easily and quickly create centers such as an art center, where students complete a drawing; a writing center, where students write a letter telling their regular teacher how the day went; a computer center, where students practice mathematics or reading skills on approved applications; a mathematics center, where students count items to put into groups of five or ten; and a reading center, where one student practices reading a story out loud to another student or a stuffed animal.

The list of possible center focuses is endless! Centers are a bit more challenging for secondary classrooms due to time constraints. For secondary classes, make your centers quick and easy: a technology center, an article read-and-share center, a visual representation (art) center, and an independent-work center, where students can work on assignments.

Partner Work

Partner work is an easy way for preK–12 students to work together, and it takes less organization than cooperative groups. Students usually really enjoy the opportunity to work with a peer. Use partner work during a lesson you provide or allow students to work together to complete an assignment after your lesson.

- **During the lesson:** Say you are teaching a full-class lesson on fractions. To help students process their learning, you might say, "Turn to the student next to you and explain to that person what an equivalent fraction is." This allows students to talk and process. Just make sure you have that "magic" signal ready to get students back together as a class.

- **Practice time after the lesson:** Say you finished the lesson and it's time for students to complete a worksheet. To allow for processing time, students could work with partners on the first five problems and then ask them to do the final five on their own.

Independent Work

Just as it sounds, students work independently and quietly on an activity. The regular teacher may include this time in the lesson plans if, for example, the teacher has students working on a writing assignment and then getting on their devices to work in a program. Be clear with your expectations for independent work so students know they cannot use this time for socializing or walking around the room. During this independent time, walk around the room checking in on individual students and monitoring behavior. Be especially clear on what students should be working on and what they can do when they are done.

Use Strategies for Success

Begin your morning by reading through the regular teacher's lesson plans, making sure technology works, ensuring you know the overall schedule of the day, and then focusing on the first part of the day. Take the day in chunks. If you are substituting in a secondary classroom, your day is naturally chunked for you in different periods. Also, remember your survival kit from chapter 1 (page 5). As a substitute teacher, you always hope for great lesson plans that are detailed and easy to follow, but some days you will simply not get a great plan from the regular teacher (or no plan at all). Your survival kit is your solution to this problem and can easily see you through a day of substituting with activities and assignments you bring with you.

Teachers greatly appreciate a substitute teacher who follows their lesson plans and tries to get most, if not all, of it done. Many teachers feel guilty for being absent, but it makes them feel so much better when they return and see the substitute teacher followed their lesson plan and students learned the material. It is hard for regular teachers to gauge how long activities and lessons will take with a substitute teacher versus when they are present. Sometimes, there will be too much to do, while other days, you will find yourself with extra time to fill. For the first problem, you and the students can only do what you can do, so you can let the teacher know in your ending note you followed the plans but were unable to complete all the activities and lessons. Teachers will understand, as timing is a tricky piece of lesson planning. If the lesson plans do not fill up the time, then go to your substitute survival kit (see page 7) and pull out activities and time fillers. For example, reading aloud to students is an easy time filler, and students of all ages enjoy being read to.

Must Do's and May Do's

A great strategy to keep students working in the classroom is to always have a list on the board of must do's and may do's. *Must do's* are assignments and work the teacher wants students to complete. Students must complete the must-do assignments and exercises before they can move on to the may do's. *May do's* are often the more student-preferred activities and therefore serve as motivation to complete the must do's. May-do activities might include drawing, silent reading, technology time on an educational application, or working in a center or with a friend.

Good Questions

One fun strategy to use in any grade-level or subject-area classroom is to use questions to help students process information, explore topics, learn about their own opinions, and learn to listen to one another. Never ask the full class a question, however. This is a rookie mistake, causing a lot of talking all at once, as students usually love to share and answer questions. Instead, set up the activity by explaining to the class you are going to ask a series of questions. Students will have time to think about their answers and then share their answers with their classmates. Make sure students know they will not be yelling out their answers! Then create some good questions that relate to what students are learning or an age-appropriate social-emotional learning lesson, such as the following activity, which is most effective with students in grade 2 and up.

Pick one or two questions and have students share their answers.

- What emoji best describes your mood right now and why?
- What is something that makes you smile at school?
- What is something you would like to learn more about and why?
- What superpower would you want the most and why?
- What is one present you hope to get in the future and why is it important?
- What is the place where you feel most yourself?
- If you could write a book about anything, what would you write about?
- What is one part of your personality you like the most?
- Would you rather work in a group or alone?
- What kind of music makes you feel happy and good?

Here are some general sample questions.

- Did you agree or disagree with what the main character in the story did?
- Would you rather live in the mountains, in the desert, or on the beach and why?
- What is your favorite thing about this school and why?
- What is your favorite subject in school and why?
- If a new student entered the classroom right now, how would you handle the situation?
- Should cell phones be allowed in upper-grade classrooms for learning purposes? Why or why not?

Once you ask the question, give students twenty seconds to think about their answer and then ask them to share with their neighbor.

The list of questions is endless. Thought-provoking questions can be fun for students to wrestle with and can also lead to great full-class discussions.

Keep a Notebook to Record Your Learning

Each day you serve as a substitute will be a learning experience. You will learn new strategies and what works and what doesn't. Keep a notebook or note your ideas on your phone. Teaching is about learning from one another, taking new

> *Speaking From Experience . . .*
> **Advice From Practicing or Former Subs**
>
> "If the regular teacher didn't leave a seating chart, quickly make one so you can call on students by name."
>
> "Never let a class go early for lunch, break, or dismissal."
>
> "Follow the teacher's lesson plan."
>
> "Praise behaviors you want to see."
>
> "Keep the students busy. Free time is an opportunity for misbehavior."

ideas, and making them yours! Before you know it, your teacher toolkit will overflow with lessons, activities, books, and ideas, and the days will fly by! As you continue to learn and grow as a guest teacher, remember this powerful quote from memoirist, poet, and civil rights activist Maya Angelou: "Do the best you can until you know better. Then when you know better, do better" (Goodreads, n.d.b). No one has to be perfect. Just do your best!

Seek Out Instructional Resources

There are many online resources available with articles, activities, and worksheets. Take some time to explore these sites and find some materials and resources you are comfortable with and can bring along with you in case you need an extra activity to get through the day. Here are a few resources for you to consider.

- Free Educational Resources (www.freeeducationalresources.com)
- ReadWorks (https://readworks.org)
- Substitute Teaching From A to Z (www.substituteteachingatoz.com)
- Education World (Sub Station: Tips and Resources for Substitute Teachers; www.educationworld.com/a_curr/curr359.shtml)
- Teacher Vision (Substitute Teacher Resources; www.teachervision.com/substitute-teacher-resources)
- ThoughtCo (How to be a Successful Substitute Teacher; https://rb.gy/dj0zv)

Use the reproducible "My Notes and Reflection" to record your thoughts about this chapter. Chapter 5 (page 51) will show you how to control what you can control.

My Notes and Reflection: Make It Manageable and Engaging

1. What are my big takeaways from this chapter?

2. What is my draft list of classroom rules I can quickly communicate to students if a class has not already established rules?

3. What engaging structures have I experienced in my own learning that I might use with students?

4. What are some activities I can prepare and have ready to go in case I have additional time with students?

5. What are some strategies I can use to gain students' attention?

6. What am I most nervous about as a guest teacher, and how can I better learn and prepare in this area so I feel more comfortable?

I Did Awesome Today!

Name of student: _____

What I did today that was great:

_____
_____
_____
_____

Substitute teacher name, signature, and comments:

_____
_____
_____
_____

Way to Go!

Super Star Award

This Super Star award is presented to

_____

for excellent behavior
and participation today!

Keep up the great work!

Super Star Award

This Super Star award is presented to

_____

for excellent behavior
and participation today!

Keep up the great work!

Oops, I Didn't Make a Good Decision Today

Name of student: _____

Time of day or period: _____

Here is what happened:

_____
_____
_____
_____

Here is why I think I didn't make a good decision:

_____
_____
_____
_____

Here is how I can make up for my poor decision:

_____
_____
_____
_____

Teacher or substitute name, signature, and date: _____

Parent signature and date: _____

The student should return this signed note to the classroom teacher.

CHAPTER 5

Stay Calm in the Storm

Despite best intentions and proactive planning, there may be times when the road gets bumpy for a substitute teacher. In fact, *all* teachers have one of "those days" from time to time. The key when this happens is the time the teacher takes to respond, reset, and refocus.

The most common challenges substitutes face usually occur in the following situations.

> **Key Points**
> - Every teacher encounters difficult days or has unsuccessful lessons.
> - The goal when things don't go as planned is to respond—not react.
> - When things get out of control, the goal is to regain control, reset, and refocus.
> - Divert, de-escalate, or redirect individual students when needed.
> - Supervising and keeping students safe are always priorities.

- The regular teacher did not provide concrete plans.
- Lesson plans are unsuccessful or there are glitches in implementation.
- Interfering or negative student behaviors derail the lesson.

Stay Calm and Respond Instead of React

Yes, we know—the phrase *stay calm* may sound flippant, but here's the real deal: *your mindset and how you respond to challenges are crucial*. It's important to realize, in most cases, challenges might not have anything to do with you. Unexpected challenges can happen to *all* teachers! Even highly experienced teachers can start a lesson and realize it isn't working or encounter student behavior that hijacks a class session. Don't see the situation as a personal reflection of your teaching abilities. Instead, do your best to view a situation objectively and realistically, asking yourself, "How might we reset this situation?" Doing so will help you respond with a plan that improves the situation instead of making it worse. Responding differs from reacting. High emotions drive a person's *reactions*, leading to hastily or poorly thought-out actions that can sometimes escalate or worsen a situation. *Responding effectively* means you've taken a moment to establish a game plan to get things back on track. Here, we'll examine how you might respond when faced with those three typical challenges and discuss strategies for moving forward.

When Concrete Plans Are Lacking

There may be times when you're subbing in a class, and the sub plans are either nonexistent or provide little to no direction. What do you do? You may have some backup activities in your survival kit (see page 7) you can implement. Following are some other ideas for setting up engaging activities for students, which ideally support their learning. You can easily adapt these backup suggestions for different grade levels or content areas.

Do some quick research before students enter the classroom, such as the following.

1. Look around the room for evidence of prior learning. Does any student work reveal a recent topic or area of learning taking place in the class?

2. Ask a neighboring teacher to share any information about the content students are currently learning.

3. As students enter, ask them what they've been learning recently.

Following are some backup lesson ideas for when concrete plans are lacking.

- **Students provide a team summary or brainstorm:** Have students produce a team summary of their learning of the topic or skill so far. You can also ask students to brainstorm why learning the skill is important or how it is applicable.

- **Students identify any unclear areas:** Ask students if there's anything in their learning they don't understand. Use the information you gain as *team challenges*, giving each team one or two questions that require members to discuss and reach agreement on the answer. Give teams time to check their notes, look for examples, and outline their answers. Then have teams each share out how they would respond to the question.

- **Students practice problems:** Check to see if there are some practice problems you can provide for students to work on. Post the problems on a whiteboard or print them. Students could also work in partner teams to solve and check their answers.

- **Students write quiz questions:** Ask teams to generate five quiz questions and answers related to their current learning within a certain amount of time. Teams each should have a member recording their work on paper or in an electronic document. After teams complete the task, ask one team to pose one of its questions to the other teams.

- **Students produce poster summaries:** Have students work in teams to graphically represent what they've learned about a topic on a whiteboard or poster paper. Teams can then do a *carousel* (also called a *gallery walk*) to view the other teams' posters and see how they describe what they learned. As students visit each poster, they can leave sticky notes about what they liked, something they would add, and so on.

- **Students participate in a chalk talk:** Gather students around a large sheet of butcher paper or the whiteboard with a single question written in the center. As this is a silent activity, have two or three markers available. For example, you may ask questions like, "What have we learned about energy?" or "How does mathematics help us in life?" Instruct students to take turns adding a comment or piece of information to the poster—no talking allowed. Students can also write comments on others' comments. Expect students to be reluctant at first, so give plenty of time for everyone to contribute.

- **Students participate in an article jigsaw:** If you have a current events article available or some other text that relates to what students are learning, divide the article text into sections and assign each section to a table group or team. Teams each are responsible for reading the information, discussing and summarizing what they learned, and then communicating what they read to the rest of the class.

> **How Would You Respond?**
>
> You arrive in a classroom and find no substitute plans. Students enter in five minutes. What is your game plan?

When Plans Are Unsuccessful or There Are Glitches in Implementation

Once in a while, a regular teacher's substitute plans aren't doable. It may be because the plans rely on technology that isn't cooperating. It may be that the lesson itself falls flat, and you can start to see students getting antsy, or you hear silence instead of student responses to your questions or comments. When facing such a challenge, remember the following *four Rs*.

- **Recognize:** Is this a technical issue (such as a technology failure), or does it relate to the activity or lesson being unsuccessful? Be aware and in touch with what's happening in the classroom. Are students getting off task or seemingly disengaging? Is there a student starting to act out? Catching situations before they go too far will help you adjust course and possibly prevent the issue from getting worse!

- **Rethink:** Breathe. Give yourself a moment to strategize how you might adjust the way you present the information or how you might improve the engagement level of students. If ideas aren't coming to you, ask students to help generate some ideas (but these ideas must be doable and appropriate). In many cases, simply switching up the structure will re-engage students (Gillyard, 2016). For example, if you're working with a whole-class structure, try using a team or small-group approach, or have students work in pairs.

- **Reset:** Implement the change. If needed, ask the class to pause or take a quick break. After the break, communicate how you will adjust the activity or lesson and the expectations for the class during that time.

- **Reflect:** Once the class is over and you have a moment to gather your thoughts, reflect on how you responded. What can you celebrate? What might you do differently next time?

How might you rethink and reset when lessons aren't working? Table 5.1 presents lesson-saver suggestions for responding when there are glitches.

> **How Would You Respond?**
>
> Everything in a teacher's daily plan depends on students accessing materials in an electronic format on the school platform. However, the entire school's internet is down. What might you do?

When Student Behaviors Derail the Lesson

Students sometimes perceive having a substitute in class as an opportunity to push the boundaries. Some students may believe you aren't aware of the rules. Other students might not see you as someone they must respect or obey.

Table 5.1: Lesson Savers

When this happens . . .	Try this . . .
Technology isn't working.	Go low-tech. If students work in teams, have them use poster paper to organize their ideas. Teams each can share what they create with the whole group.
	Have students do a quick write-in response to a compelling question you write on the board that relates to their lesson. Have students share their responses in pairs, then groups of four, then eight.
	Have students generate a list of all the things they would do if they didn't have access to technology for a month. Have them share their top two things with a table group or partners.
	Use backup activities from your survival kit or those we list in this chapter (chalk talk, poster summaries, and so on; see page 52).
	Read a current events article (that ideally connects to a similar topic) and divide students into discussion groups.
Students aren't engaging in or responding to the lesson.	Take a brain break. Play some music or use another strategy to give students a break for a specific timeframe. Make age-appropriate choices.
	Divide students into small groups (three or four students) and ask them to process the information by answering the following questions. • "What are we learning?" • "What are some key vocabulary words that relate to what we are learning?" • "Why is what we are learning important?" • "What questions come to mind about what we are learning?" • "If we had to teach someone this information, how would we do it?"
	Give teams poster paper and markers. Ask them to create a visual illustration of the process or information you're teaching.
	Use backup activities from your survival kit or those we list in this chapter (chalk talk, poster summaries, and so on; see page 52).
Most students are demonstrating a lack of understanding about a process or concept (for example, in mathematics), and don't seem able to complete an assigned task (as planned).	Provide more instruction about the process.
	Divide the task into small steps. Ask students to complete the first step, and then have students share out how they approach the task. Continue with the next steps.
	Look for successful student examples from the class and ask permission to share. If a student is uncomfortable sharing the example, ask if you can share without disclosing the student's name. Have the class share what they think is effective about the work or what they notice. Have them look at their own work.

Some students may demonstrate a lack of compliance or unwillingness to engage in the lesson. When a student acts out, your response is key. While we can't capture every possible scenario and solution in this book, there are some helpful guidelines you can use to divert, de-escalate, or redirect individual students when needed.

First, here are some general guidelines for working with challenging students.

- Pick your battles. Don't engage in trying to correct inconsequential behaviors.
- Make sure you clarified expectations with the student.
- Remain calm and professional.
- Confront the student privately. Most students will respond to you chatting with them one-to-one, but will react strongly if you confront them in front of their classmates.
- Provide a chance for the student to follow through with redirection and acknowledge your appreciation when the student does.
- Do not make physical contact with a student unless not doing so risks someone's safety.

Divert Challenging Behavior

Ideally, you will recognize warning signs or signals when a student's behavior is escalating, so your efforts will decrease the likelihood for things to get out of control. For example, a student might begin to tap a pencil loudly, or start to poke a nearby student. The student may be seeking attention or trying to get out of doing a task. Your goal is to find a way to re-engage students who seem to be veering off task and keep them busy. For example, you might give students in need of diversion a job passing out papers, or ask them to assist another student with the assigned task.

Adjust Your Language to De-Escalate

How you verbally interact with students who exhibit challenging behavior can either escalate or de-escalate a situation. Look at how people state the same message differently when playing telephone (page 10)—one way is likely to escalate behavior and another, de-escalate it, as in the following examples.

- "Why do you have your phone out? I told you to put it away."
- "My friends, this activity does not allow you to use phones, so I need you to put yours away. I would hate this to be an issue for anyone. Thanks—I appreciate it."

The first message puts students on the defensive, asking them why they have violated the rule. The second message simply states the rule and your expectation.

As a general rule, try to phrase things positively. You might even take the student aside and explain you're trying to make sure the class is successful and really need the student's help.

Avoid the Power Struggle

One never knows a student's whole story—perhaps the student had a difficult morning at home or is experiencing some other challenge. When you see a student starting to shut down, don't engage in a power struggle. Move on. Pushing students into compliance when they are only going to push back and escalate the situation offers little to gain; it becomes a *power struggle* with no winner. Rather than insisting the student comply, potentially escalating the situation, give the student some time to regroup. You can quietly say, "I can see you need a little time to think right now. I can let you have that time, provided you're not interrupting anyone or the class. Let me know when you're ready to return to the activity."

If you have a student confront you with an "in your face" question such as, "What are you going to do about it?" don't feel you need to respond with an answer immediately. You have the right to take a moment by saying, "I'm going to have to think about how I would like to answer that question. I'll get back to you." This reduces the likelihood you'll get into a power struggle.

Redirect Negative Behavior

Sometimes students have more behavioral challenges during whole-class activities than when doing activities in small groups or teams. You can use this knowledge and harness the *power of peers* to redirect a student's behavior. For example, you might divide the class into smaller groups and give students a task to complete as a team. Often, the student will respond more appropriately with peers than the student would when you give a directive or ask the student to work independently. For instance, if a class is studying a particular topic, you can create a team competition in which teams list as many facts or pieces of information about that topic they can in ten minutes. While the teams work, move around the room and check in periodically to ensure the student in question is participating and contributing.

> **How Would You Respond?**
>
> When you ask a student to work on the assignment, the student refuses, stating, "I don't need to listen to you. You're not my teacher." What might you do?

Reflect on Your Challenging Experiences

You've made it through the storm! It helps to take time to ask yourself, "What did I learn from this experience? What can I celebrate? What might I do differently next time?"

We hope this chapter provides some ideas to use when things don't go according to plan. By having some of these strategies in mind, you're less likely to be caught off guard and unable to problem solve. Use the reproducible "My Notes and Reflection" to record your thoughts about this chapter. Chapter 6 (page 61) provides suggestions for how you can take care of yourself when you've had a rough day and also shares some ideas for ending your day as a substitute in a manner that celebrates your accomplishments and is informative and helpful to the regular teacher.

Speaking From Experience . . .
Advice From Practicing or Former Subs

"If an activity has gone badly, let the class know the next activity provides a fresh start."

"Avoid confrontations that can lead to a situation where a student feels the need to 'save face.'"

"If a situation is truly something beyond your control, call the office for assistance."

"Do not tolerate name-calling or rudeness among students."

My Notes and Reflection: Stay Calm in the Storm

1. What are my big takeaways from this chapter?

2. What can I do to remember to respond instead of react when things don't go according to plan?

3. How might I positively communicate a reset with students when things don't seem to be working? What words might I choose?

4. In my own learning experiences, what go-to structures did I find engaging that I might also use with students if plans go off course?

5. Are there any additional ideas I would add to my backup plan when classroom plans don't work out?

CHAPTER 6

End Strong

Your day is done! The final bell rings! You experience a mixture of excitement, relief, reflection, and exhaustion. Your mind quickly transitions to what you need to be moving on to in your own life. Errands, exercise, or many other activities fill your personal to-do list. But before you jump back into your personal life, we detail

> **Key Points**
> - It is important to leave the classroom better than you found it.
> - Leave a note for the returning classroom teacher explaining how the day went.
> - After a day of substitute teaching, it is important to focus on intentional self-care.

in this chapter a few more tasks to finish before school personnel will consider you a top substitute teacher. Luckily, these tasks don't take much time, but they leave a huge positive impression!

Reflect on What You Learned

Take a moment to reflect on the day. What went well, and what was challenging? Did you learn anything new? Did you learn anything from the regular teacher's classroom or lesson plans? Did you learn any new ideas to take with you into your substitute future? Jot those ideas in your notes app or a notebook, along with any other learnings from the day.

Tidy Up the Classroom

Just as a guest would do, take a few minutes to leave the classroom as clean (or cleaner) than you found it. You will truly be a hero by doing this! When teachers are out sick, they might return the next day tired and still not feeling like themselves. When they walk into a neat and organized classroom, it is such a relief! Pick up and straighten the desks. Erase the whiteboard where it makes sense to, and ensure you have all your personal belongings.

Leave a Note for the Teacher

This is a critical task when substituting. Teachers want to know how the day went and how much of the lesson plans you and the students completed. They also want to know how their students behaved and generally what went on throughout the day. Here are the main points to cover in your note to regular (returning) teachers.

- Welcome them back and thank them for having you.
- Give an overall report of the day. Tell them how the day went in general.
- Describe progress with lessons. Explain how you were able to follow their lesson plans and what you and the students completed or didn't complete. If you had a printed lesson plan to follow for the day, you can write on the plan or leave sticky notes on it with details of how each part of the day went.
- Make a list of students who were helpful.
- Make a list of students who had challenging behavior and how you handled them. (Leave a copy of the reproducible "Oops, I Didn't Make a Good Decision Today," page 50, if applicable.)
- Provide miscellaneous important information. For example, was there a fire drill, or did a parent ask a question about an upcoming field trip during drop-off?
- Write an ending note. Let teachers know if you would like them to invite you back and leave your substitute information for them.

Figure 6.1 shows an example of a note to a teacher.

If you prefer a simple form, see the reproducible "End-of-Day Report From Your Substitute Teacher" (page 71), which you can print and complete before leaving for the day. It is important that whatever form you use, you don't include any confidential information or use the note to vent after a challenging day. Instead, just report the facts without a lot of emotion. The regular teachers will take care of the rest when they return.

> Dear Mrs. Chandler,
>
> We had a great day! Thank you for the detailed lesson plans you provided. We were able to accomplish all the assignments except for the final science assignment, as we ran out of time. I did assign the homework you wanted the students to do this evening and went over it in detail with the students. The Character Counts assembly was very well done, and the students greatly enjoyed attending. They wanted to discuss what they had learned when we returned to class, and we had a powerful conversation about the importance of developing one's character and having integrity. Several students who were extremely helpful and responsible were Bradley, Serena, Jose, and Jackie. I did have to redirect Tim and Estrella several times throughout the day. I would love to sub for you again in the future. My number is 101.202.3003, or I can be reached at thebestsubever@email.com. Thank you again for this wonderful opportunity!
>
> Sincerely,
>
> Mr. Jones

Figure 6.1: Sample end-of-day note for the returning classroom teacher.

Check Out in the Office

Once you reflect on the day, clean up the classroom, and leave your note for the returning teacher, it is time to lock up the classroom and head to the office. Turn in your key and anything else the office staff gave you that morning. Make sure to let the staff know how much you enjoyed being at their school and hope to return. You can always leave your card with them as well. Leave with a smile on your face. Everyone loves a happy substitute! If you are a long-term sub, check with the office manager to find out if you need to check in and out of the office each day. Some schools will want you to while others may have you keep the classroom key and not do a formal check-in or check-out process. If that is the case, make sure to stop by the office in the morning and again in the afternoon to check the regular teacher's inbox for any mail and say goodbye.

> ### *Do This* Scenario
>
> Ms. Rodriguez had a good day subbing in a fifth-grade classroom. The students are gone, and she is looking forward to enjoying an afternoon hike in the hills above her home. She looks around the classroom and sees not all students followed her directions to clean up their desk and area. She glances at her watch and knows the afternoon light is fleeting. She also knows she wants a great reputation as a substitute. She spends the next ten minutes straightening the desks and picking up trash. She tidies the front desk area of the classroom and cleans off the whiteboard. She then heads to the front office, where the office manager comments, "Oh, you are still here!" After explaining she wanted to make sure the classroom was clean and tidy for the classroom teacher to return to, the office manager says, "I wish more subs were like you! I will keep your name and number and hope to see you again." Finishing the day strong gives you peace of mind that you did the job well.
>
> ### *Don't Do This* Scenario
>
> The day is done! Mr. Lewis is looking forward to getting home and taking his dog for a long walk. He walks his students to the exit of the school and returns to a messy classroom, where students did not clean up after the last activity. Mr. Lewis says to himself, "I can't believe kids these days. I shouldn't have to remind them to clean up." Mr. Lewis picks up a few big pieces of trash on the floor, quickly erases the board, and heads out of the classroom. He stops by the office on the way out, leaving the key and sub folder with the first person he sees—even though it's not the person who usually checks the subs in and out. Without saying much, he heads out the door to get home. As Mr. Lewis is getting in his car, he sees the office manager collecting the sub folder and key from the front desk clerk. She looks outside, sees Mr. Lewis at his car, shakes her head, and walks away. Mr. Lewis doesn't even realize his reputation has just taken a hit that will be hard to recover from.

Care for Yourself

Guest teaching is hard work. Teachers make 1,500 educational decisions a day and four educational decisions *each minute* (TeachThought Staff, 2016)! In addition, administrators expect teachers to be role models, counselors, foster parents, assessors, information providers, discipline controllers, and more. It is exhausting just to read the list! So why do people choose to teach or become a guest teacher? Usually, they mention the rewards that come with helping students and the joy they find in a classroom. Regardless of the joy and rewards of teaching, it is essential to acknowledge this job requires a lot of interpersonal skills and interactions and can be draining and exhausting, which is why guest teachers must be intentional in their care for themselves.

Self-care advocacy has a larger presence in contemporary society. While people once considered *self-care* a trip to the spa or getting your nails done, the definition transformed into an intentional way of living life that prioritizes your own care. The increasing amount of anxiety and stress people experience in their daily lives fuels self-care, which has become a mainstream idea that continues gathering momentum. Research links prioritizing self-care to being more productive and happier, as the National Council for Mental Well-Being shares.

> Engaging in a self-care routine has been clinically proven to reduce or eliminate anxiety and depression, reduce stress, increase happiness, and more. It can help you adapt to changes, build strong relationships, and recover from setbacks. In a national survey, Americans cited benefits of self-care as: enhanced self-confidence (64%), increased productivity (67%), and happiness (71%) (as cited in Eat Smart, Move More, n.d.).

Those outstanding statistics definitely back up the importance of focusing on self-care! Alyssa F. Westring (2021), the Vincent de Paul professor and chair of the Department of Management and Entrepreneurship at DePaul University's Driehaus College of Business, adds:

> Making the time for self-care is essential to performing well in all the other areas of our lives. Ample research has shown that nurturing our brains, bodies, and spirits can help us be more effective at whatever we put our minds to.

Find Your Own Self-Care Routine

There is no "right" way to do self-care (Westring, 2021). Self-care activities can be small or large, with examples ranging from packing a healthy lunch to waking up early every day to do a mindfulness meditation before work. Self-care looks different for everyone! What one person considers self-care may include a long walk and a favorite television show. Another person may find self-care in turning off the phone and journaling. It really depends on what makes you exhale and come back into the present moment. Take time to notice what makes you relax and which self-care activities do not resonate with you. Try small, doable activities that are not overwhelming. It is all about what makes you relax and rejuvenate.

There is a lot of well-meaning advice about self-care coming at teachers on a daily basis. Only you can determine what self-care activities and habits work for you. It is exciting to try different activities and routines to identify what works best for you. Here are a few suggestions on how to care for yourself during your guest teaching career.

Make Time to Rest and Renew

Teaching can be socially draining. Plan at least ten to twenty minutes a day when you can take a break and enjoy some alone time. Take a walk around the school building (or even take a few laps around your classroom) over your lunch break, fill your water bottle throughout the day, or sit in your car or at your desk and listen to your favorite song. Taking time to do some mindfulness and relaxation techniques can be very calming as well. When you get home, get off your feet for a while, and enjoy some peace and quiet.

In their article "The Science of Resting (Well)," coauthors Tomas Chamorro-Premuzic and Sunny Lee (2022) point out the importance of resting and how resting is different for different people:

> We all know that it is important to rest. Research has shown that resting is vital to humans' mental and physical health, given its great benefits to our immune system, stress management, mood, decision-making, creativity, and work productivity. However, what is less known is *how to rest well*.

Chamorro-Premuzic and Lee (2022) also make suggestions on what it may mean to *rest well*.

- Schedule downtime and make it a routine so it becomes a daily habit.
- Find the right amount of rest—not enough and too much rest can both have a negative impact on performance.
- Identify and prioritize your specific needs. Find your own way to rest. Not all rest activities are passive. For example, walking may not be a good type of rest for those who are physically exhausted, but walking, especially in nature, can be a good way to restore emotional and mental energy.
- Don't skip your vacation. Longer periods of time to rest and rejuvenate are necessary.

Making time to rest and rejuvenate will help you stay healthy, strong, and ready for your next day as a guest teacher!

Get Enough Sleep

What about sleep? Research illuminates the importance of getting enough sleep and keeping your sleep pattern regular. In their American Academy of Sleep Medicine position statement, sleep medicine specialist Kannan Ramar and colleagues (2021) note:

> Sleep is vital for health and well-being in children, adolescents, and adults. Healthy sleep is important for cognitive functioning, mood, mental health, and cardiovascular, cerebrovascular, and metabolic health. Adequate quantity and quality of sleep also play a role in reducing the risk of accidents and injuries caused by sleepiness and fatigue.

These experts go on to recommend the average adult sleep seven or more hours per night, and share that the National Sleep Foundation recommends seven to nine hours per night (Ramar, et al., 2021).

Guest teachers need their sleep! The job requires an early wake-up call and may cause you to have to adjust your nighttime routine. Remember, you will get back that time in the afternoon once school is over, and you had enough sleep to enjoy the day!

Keep a Journal

Log both your good and bad experiences. Writing is an amazing way to process and work through emotions on challenging days. If you're feeling overwhelmed, look up previous positive experiences to bring a smile to your face. Remember, you are the only one who will see your writing, so don't be afraid to be honest with yourself. In an article titled "Journaling for Mental Health," the University of Rochester Medical Center (2023) posits:

> One of the ways to deal with any overwhelming emotion is to find a healthy way to express yourself. This makes a journal a helpful tool in managing your mental health. Journaling can help you:
> - Manage anxiety
> - Reduce stress
> - Cope with depression

Journaling helps provide an opportunity to increase positive self-talk and prioritize concerns and problems (University of Rochester Medical Center, 2023). Get a journal and give it a try!

Create a Circle of Social Support

There are many benefits of building social support in your life. According to the American Psychological Association (2022):

> Almost all of us benefit from social and emotional support. And though it may seem counterintuitive, having strong social support can actually make you more able to cope with problems on your own, by improving your self-esteem and sense of autonomy.

You don't need an extensive network of support people—even a few good friends or colleagues can make a huge difference by providing you with an outlet to talk and spend quality time. After being around students all day, be sure to schedule some adult time with friends and family.

Take Care of Yourself Physically

Evidence shows regular physical activity increases energy and reduces your risk of health problems, adding the following five benefits of exercise (Harvard Health Publishing, 2022):

1. It counteracts the effects of weight-promoting genes.
2. It helps tame a sweet tooth.
3. It reduces the risk of developing breast cancer.
4. It eases joint pain.
5. It boosts immune function.

Movement can also be a fun way to release stress and give you time to think and process. Walking is a simple yet highly effective way to get movement into your daily routine. Gardening, bike riding, jogging, and playing pickleball are just a few others. The important thing is to move and keep moving!

Take Time Off When Needed

A crucial aspect of self-care is managing stress and taking breaks when necessary. This is when being in control of your schedule is a bonus! Decide not to accept jobs and plan a personal day or two to focus on self-care and get out in nature or run errands. Harvard Business School professor Leslie A. Perlow and research associate Jessica L. Porter (2009) write that rest actually *improves* your performance. When people have predictable and consistent time off work, they are actually more productive overall because they feel more mentally rested, which increases motivation and work enjoyment.

So don't feel bad for taking the days off you need to have a balanced and healthy life. It will make you a better guest teacher in the end!

Nurture Your Hobbies and Interests

One of the great things about working in the education system is the holiday and summer breaks. Take advantage of the schedule and learn or practice new hobbies during your time off. Pick up golf or art, take an afternoon writing class, learn how to cook, or read a good book. Blogger Ren Wu (2022) offers these six reasons to focus on your hobbies:

1. You can spend your time doing something you enjoy
2. You'll challenge yourself and grow in the process
3. Hobbies help take care of your mental health
4. You'll feel less stress
5. You'll find purpose and freedom in your free time
6. It will be easier to find new friends and relationships

By planning an activity or hobby to look forward to, your "teacher brain" gets to turn off and rest, and you get to be the kid and go play!

Remember to Start Fresh Every Day

Each day is a new and fresh start. Approach each day with positivity and the knowledge that whatever comes your way today, you will be able to handle and even enjoy it. You are resilient and strong—nothing keeps a great sub down!

Ending your day strong and adding regular self-care routines will make it easier to be ready for another great day of work as a guest teacher. Use the reproducible "My Notes and Reflection" (page 70) to record your thoughts about this chapter. Check out the reproducible "End-of-Day Report From Your Substitute Teacher" (page 71) to see if you might want to use it in your daily wrap-up work. As you gain more experience as a guest teacher, you'll discover it might be time to grow into the next phase of your career; chapter 7 (page 73) will help you get started on your next steps.

Speaking From Experience . . .
Advice From Practicing or Former Subs

"If the teacher has a classroom set (of books, Chromebooks, calculators, and so on), make sure students return them before the entire class leaves or at the end of the day."

"Teachers really appreciate having feedback on your experience so they can follow up accordingly with students and get insights on their own preparation."

My Notes and Reflection: End Strong

1. What are my big takeaways from this chapter?

2. How can I best support the regular classroom teacher after my sub day is done?

3. What are some ways I can renew my own energy so I can be healthy and fresh?

End-of-Day Report From Your Substitute Teacher

Substitute teacher: _____

Regular teacher: _____

Students absent: _____

General comments:

_____

_____

_____

Assignments completed:

_____

_____

_____

Assignments unable to complete:

_____

_____

_____

Helpful students:

_____

_____

_____

Challenging students:

_____

_____

_____

The Successful Substitute © 2024 Solution Tree Press • SolutionTree.com
Visit **go.SolutionTree.com/teacherefficacy** to download this free reproducible.

CHAPTER 7

Thrive and Grow Into Your Future

Substitute teaching provides a lot of opportunities for both personal and professional growth. Some people enjoy substitute teaching as a part-time job as they pursue other hobbies and interests. Others use substitute teaching as their main source of income, while others use it to catapult themselves into full-time teaching jobs. Whatever your pathway, growing and learning through this career can be very satisfying and enjoyable.

Key Points

- Substitute teachers often consider options for expanding to long-term substitute teaching or other pathways in education.
- There are an increasing number of options for attaining teaching credentials.
- Regardless of your future career, your experiences as a substitute will build valuable skills you can include in your résumé and cover letter.

As you grow as a substitute teacher, you will become very aware of the many different professions in the education field. Instructional aides in the classroom, student supervisors, office staff, and custodial staff all keep a school site running smoothly. You may wonder what your next steps are, and in this chapter, we discuss a few options.

Preparation Activities

Before deciding your next steps, here are suggestions for preparation activities to do so you can be ready for that next chapter in your career.

- Keep your résumé updated with your substitute teaching experiences, particularly those that are unique. Put together a small portfolio of any artifacts you created during extended or long-term assignments, such as unit plans. Show some of the student work from these artifacts.

- Be sure to monitor open positions at the schools where you enjoy working.

- Participate in professional development whenever possible, including participation in collaborative team meetings (which typically take place during the school day).

- If you have a chance, observe a veteran teacher's classroom to gain strategies and see the techniques in action (check with the principal first to make sure it's OK).

Long-Term Substitute Teaching

After subbing in daily jobs and moving from school to school, many district leaders ask experienced substitute teachers to take on long-term substitute teaching jobs, which can be one week to several months long. Many districts also post openings for long-term substitute teachers for which you can apply. Some districts have additional requirements for long-term subs, like having a teaching credential or taking some additional courses. The job descriptions will explain these requirements, so read them carefully.

Long-term substitute teaching is a great way to add consistency to your days, and you become the daily teacher. Students get to know you, and the classroom becomes where you belong. You continue to follow the overall plans the regular classroom teacher left for you, but you can also add a few more of your own activities you and the students may enjoy as well.

Since you will be responsible for being the main teacher for a period of time, it is vital you spend time studying the curriculum and standards for that grade level or subject area. You will be responsible for student assessment, parent communications, and disciplining students. Try to gain as much information as possible about the students, parents, and anything else related to the school routines from the outgoing teacher. If the teacher has already left, find another teacher at the same grade level or one who works close by to ask questions to and gain information from. The more questions you can ask up front, the more information you will have to be a successful long-term substitute teacher. Here is a list of possible questions you may want to ask.

- "What students are the natural leaders in the classroom I can trust to give accurate and honest information?"
- "Are there any students with special needs (such as learning disabilities, health issues, and so on) I need to be aware of to meet their needs?"
- "Are there students who need additional support for their behavior? If so, what types of strategies have been successful?"
- "Are there parent volunteers who come into the classroom to help? On which days and times? What tasks do they help with?"
- "Are there emergency drills or safety routines I should be aware of at the school?"
- "What am I responsible for teaching on a daily basis?"
- "Are there assessments and evaluations I need to give to students?"
- "How should I record student grades?"
- "What types of parent communications am I responsible for?"
- "Do I have duties around the school (outside the classroom)?"
- "Where should I park?"
- "What is the daily schedule?"
- "Are there students who leave to go to another classroom for services during the day?"
- "What are the safety procedures at the school? For fire drills?"
- "What is the classroom-management plan for behavior issues? Rewards?"
- "Are there schoolwide events or assemblies I need to be aware of?"
- "Should I check in with the office or other teachers on a regular basis?"

Long-term subbing gives you an excellent opportunity to explore what it is like to be a full-time teacher. You can enjoy putting your own creativity into your classroom plans and assignments. It is also a perfect way to continue to grow as a substitute teacher.

Your Teaching Credentials

After substitute teaching for a while, you may feel *a calling* (that is, a vocation or a passion) to become a classroom teacher. We know from experience, many teachers start as substitute teachers and realize their next step is pursuing full-time teaching. Each state has different teaching credential requirements, so do your research and find out what they are. Generally, most U.S. states offer the following three different credentials.

1. Multiple subject, elementary level
2. Single subject, secondary level
3. Special education, all levels

It is important to note that many private schools do not require a teaching credential to teach at their school. If you are interested in that option, visit the school's website and contact the office to express your interest.

Next, find a program that fits your life and budget. There are so many different teaching credential programs—at your local university and online. Most public and private universities offer teaching credential programs that require an additional year of classes and student teaching. There are also many online teaching credential programs.

Most programs offer in-person and online courses geared toward working professionals. Most states do require student teaching as a prerequisite to obtaining your teaching credential. Check with your state's teacher credentialing office to ensure you have the most updated information and requirements. Visit Teacher Certification Degrees (www.teachercertificationdegrees.com/reciprocity) to see requirements for each U.S. state. U.S. states also work together to assist teachers certificated in one state who move to another state to teach. This partnership is called *reciprocity* and is critically needed due to shortages in the teaching ranks. Some states have greatly reduced or eliminated additional classes and other requirements since the COVID-19 pandemic (Reilly, 2021).

Speaking From Experience . . .
Advice From Practicing or Former Subs

> "When I first began subbing, I thought it would be a short-term experience. Little did I know I would fall in love with teaching. I'm now in my seventh year as a full-time teacher!"

A major benefit of substituting before becoming a full-time teacher is you experience many different classrooms, schools, and districts. This can help you identify which grade levels, subject areas, schools, and districts you would be interested in. Let administrators in the schools know you are interested and are pursuing your teaching degree; many times, principals will prefer to hire a substitute teacher they know and have seen teach over someone unfamiliar to them. Use your subbing experience as your superpower!

Sample Résumé and Cover Letter

As you prepare to seek employment either as a long-term substitute or permanent full-time teacher, start by updating your résumé and writing a strong cover letter. Your résumé should not be longer than two pages and your cover letter, one page. There are many great resources online to help you create a résumé and cover letter, such as the following.

- Resume Builder (www.resumebuilder.com)
- Zety (https://zety.com/resume-builder)
- My Perfect Resume (www.myperfectresume.com)

A sample résumé (see figure 7.1) and cover letter (see figure 7.2, page 78) will help you get started if your next step involves applying at school districts for open full-time teaching positions. This is not a time to be humble! Recognize your hard work, ability to work well with others, and other special or unique qualities that make you stand out. Add them to your résumé and write a cover letter that illuminates your skills and qualities.

Mark Best Substitute
1212 Teacher Lane
Mulberry, TX 94332
890-456-5432

Substitute teacher with more than two years of successful experience and a proven record of providing highly engaging lessons and activities for students of all ages. Strong in technology, mathematics, and interpersonal skills, as well as highly organized and a team player. Passionate about education and youth.

PROFESSIONAL EXPERIENCE
Substitute Teacher
North Unified School District, North City, CA
August 2021–Present
- Consistently performs substitute teacher assignments on a daily basis
- Substitute teaches in K–8 classes covering numerous subjects
- Uses technology to engage students and perform substitute teaching duties
- Collaborates with regular teachers in developing lesson plans and activities
- Is punctual on a daily basis and volunteers for additional duties as needed

Additional Work
- Private tutor—Tutored students ages seven to ten in reading and mathematics
- Jamba Juice clerk—Assisted customers with orders and preparing food and drink items
- Fast food server—Worked at Taco Bell as a server and food preparer

EDUCATION
- San Diego State University, San Diego, California May 2022, Master's in education with a multiple-subject teaching credential
- May 2021, Bachelor's in arts communication studies

ADDITIONAL SKILLS
Flexible, positive, organized, problem solver, team player, tech savvy, strong communicator, experienced, quick learner

Figure 7.1: Sample résumé format.

Mark Best Substitute
1212 Teacher Lane
Mulberry, TX 94332
890-456-5432

Dear Dr. Abbot,

I am writing to express my interest in the position of an elementary teacher in your school district. With over two years of experience in elementary education, I have the skills to join your team of amazing educators and contribute to the continued success of your school district.

Currently, I am a successful substitute teacher in your district and have greatly enjoyed learning and growing my instructional abilities. I have subbed in classrooms from preschool through tenth grade and have enjoyed all ages and subjects. My classroom-management skills are strong, as is my ability to foster constructive learning environments.

Some of the unique skills I will bring to this position include the following.

- Technology skills—I am extremely comfortable with technology, software programs, and social media.
- Mathematics strength—I am able to teach complex mathematics concepts to students with clarity.
- Team player—My background in athletics and membership in organizations has taught me the skills it takes to have a good relationship with a wide range of people and be a contributing member of the group.
- Passion—I am passionate about education and students, and will bring this passion to the classroom every day.

I am excited by the prospect of working for your school district!

I look forward to the opportunity to interview for this position.

Sincerely,

Mark Best Substitute

Figure 7.2: Sample cover letter format.

It is an exciting time to be a teacher—a job with a lot of purpose and variety. This chapter looked at options that open up once you have been substitute teaching for a few months or years. It is up to you if you want to be a more permanent employee at a school site or if you prefer to continue to move from school to school. Each option has benefits and challenges. Either way, there are many ways to continue to grow as a guest teacher. Use the reproducible "My Notes and Reflection" to record your thoughts about this chapter. Chapter 8 (page 81) highlights some of these growth opportunities.

My Notes and Reflection: Thrive and Grow Into Your Future

1. What are my big takeaways from this chapter?

2. What do I need to add to update my résumé?

3. What are the pros and cons of taking a long-term substitute job?

4. Do I have any interest in pursuing a teaching credential?

CHAPTER 8

Keep Going! Keep Growing!

Key Points
- Reflect on your experiences as a guest teacher.
- Find suggestions for resources to keep you growing and learning.

We wrote this book to give you practical information and ideas to think about when substitute teaching. The better prepared you are, the easier it will be for you to take jobs without too much stress or worry. By even having this book in your hand, you are better prepared and ready to teach. This chapter is a reminder of some of the most practical points of substitute teaching.

There is a lot to remember. You don't have to master it all at once—take it one day at a time, learn through trial and error, talk to other educators, and be kind to yourself. Remember, the more you guest teach, the better you will be at guest teaching.

Some of the big ideas in this book include those traits and habits successful guest teachers use daily. They prepare, show up early, and are flexible. They have a good relationship with the school staff and add value by being responsible. They follow lesson plans and are warm to students, while also providing a structured environment. They end the day strong, with a clean classroom and a note for the regular teacher. They use self-care strategies to renew so they are ready for the next day's challenges. They deal with these challenges and enjoy the daily joys of the job.

Being a guest teacher can be challenging and extremely rewarding at the same time. Focus on the parts of the job you love and find joy in, and do your best to ignore the challenging moments—every job has them. This job is made for those who like to be physically busy and not confined to a desk. Guest teaching has its own element of freedom, and once you open that classroom door, *you are the boss*. This is critical to remember and will help you take ownership in your career as a guest teacher.

Soft Skills Count

Guest teaching is great preparation for many other jobs. Getting to know students of different ages will help if you are a parent or become one in your future. Say your life takes you in a completely different direction and you find yourself in a large business. Your ability to speak with clarity, presence, and an empowering voice will serve you well. Guest teaching strengthens your *soft skills* (like communication and social awareness) and your ability to work with a wide range of individuals. Employers recognize the importance of soft skills in the workplace, so it's important to showcase these skills when applying for jobs (KnowledgeHut, 2023). Soft skills show employers your personal attributes and qualities that will help you succeed—like your ability to problem solve, be creative, and show integrity (KnowledgeHut, 2023). Being a guest teacher polishes these and other soft skills such as clear communication, working well with others, and being responsible. This job prepares you for future work, whether in education or other fields, and will make you a more well-rounded individual. After all, if you can be a guest teacher to thirty students who aren't related to you, you can do anything!

The exciting part of being a guest teacher is the job stretches you out of your safety zone and forces you to grow and learn. As psychologist Abraham H. Maslow (1966) said, "One can choose to go back toward safety or forward toward growth. Growth must be chosen again and again; fear must be overcome again and again." To keep growing, the next section offers some online and print resources to use in your next steps as an educator.

Resources to Keep Learning

The end of this book does not mean the end of your learning process! In fact, you could consider this only the beginning. There is a wealth of information online to help you continue to learn the craft of guest teaching, as well as dive deeper into content knowledge. Some of these websites worth a visit include the following.

- Cybrary Man's Educational Web Sites (www.cybraryman.com) is a database of websites related to teaching.
- Education World (www.educationworld.com) offers educational resources and activities.

- Edutopia (https://edutopia.org) features teaching articles and videos on many topics.
- Go Noodle (https://gonoodle.com) is full of movement and mindfulness videos for the perfect brain break.
- Kahoot! (www.kahoot.com) allows you to create a trivia quiz or learning game on any subject.
- Khan Academy (www.khanacademy.org) provides a wealth of information and online lessons for every content area.
- Quizlet (www.Quizlet.com) has a tool to browse or create online flashcards.
- Storyboard That (www.storyboardthat.com) is a tool to create storyboards that bring your lessons to life.
- Teaching Channel (www.teachingchannel.com) is a one-stop shop for teacher learning and development.
- Teacher Vision (www.teachervision.com) offers print-ready and digital resources for teachers.
- TedEd (https://ed.ted.com/educator) features Ted Talks that focus on education themes.

Here are some of our all-time favorite educator books that make great next steps for your learning and growth.

- *The New Art and Science of Teaching* by Robert J. Marzano (2017): This book, based on Marzano's fifty years of education research, provides practical instructional strategies teachers can use immediately in the classroom.
- *Embracing Relational Teaching: How Strong Relationships Promote Student Self-Regulation and Efficacy* by Anthony R. Reibel (2023): Shifting from transactional to relational teaching empowers students and creates a more engaging classroom environment. *Transactional teaching* is when the to-do list rules; teachers are busy teaching lessons and assigning activities without much concern for students' thoughts and feelings. *Relational teaching* is when teachers take time to build relationships with students and know their interests; teachers use these relationships to strengthen teaching and learning in the classroom. This book explores the *why* behind this shift and shares applicable strategies for K–12 teachers.

- *Designing Effective Classroom Management* by Jason E. Harlacher (2015): With this practical, step-by-step guide, teachers and school administrators will learn five components that help improve student achievement and reduce classroom problems.
- *The Highly Engaged Classroom* by Robert J. Marzano and Debra J. Pickering (2011): Key research and practical strategies enable all teachers to create a classroom environment where engagement is the norm, not the exception.
- *Teach Like a Champion 2.0: 62 Techniques That Put Students on the Path to College* by Doug Lemov (2015): This book provides very practical classroom techniques and strategies for K–12 teachers.
- *Better Learning Through Structured Teaching: A Framework for the Gradual Release of Responsibility* by Douglas Fisher and Nancy Frey (2014): A wonderful resource to help teachers design instructional routines that start with the teacher but work toward releasing the responsibility of the work to the student.

Enjoy the Ride

As we wrap up this book, we hope you remember all who teach are unique individuals who bring something special to the classroom. Prepare, trust your instincts, and then enjoy the ride! Each day in a classroom will have times of fun and joy as well as unexpected situations. Find the humor in working with students and the joy of working at a school site that harnesses the special energy in ways only educators can. Primatologist and anthropologist Jane Goodall once said, "What you do makes a difference, and you have to decide what kind of difference you want to make" (Goodreads, n.d.a). Being a guest teacher does make a difference in the lives of young people. Find your unique way of connecting and teaching, and be true to your own ideas and voice. By doing so, you will truly make a difference! You have embarked on a fun, active, challenging, and satisfying job. Good luck and have some fun out there!

References and Resources

American Psychological Association. (2022, October 21). *Manage stress: Strengthen your support network*. Accessed at https://apa.org/topics/stress/manage-social-support#:~:text=Experts%20 say%20that%20almost%20all,esteem%20and%20sense%20of%20autonomy. on August 16, 2023.

Center for Teaching Innovation. (2023). *Collaborative learning*. Accessed at https://teaching.cornell.edu/teaching-resources/active-collaborative-learning/collaborative-learning on July 17, 2023.

Chamorro-Premuzic, T., & Lee, S. (2022, October 14). *The science of resting (well)*. Accessed at www.fastcompany.com/90795521/science-of-resting-well on July 25, 2023.

Cook, C. R., Coco, S., Zhang, Y., Fiat, A. E., Duong, M. T., Renshaw, T. L., et al. (2018). Cultivating positive teacher-student relationships: Preliminary evaluation of the establish–maintain–restore (EMR) method. *School Psychology Review, 47*(3), 226–243. Accessed at https://doi.org/10.17105/spr-2017-0025.v47-3 on October 27, 2023.

Eat Smart, Move More. (n.d.). *What is self-care? Tips and practices* [Blog post]. Accessed at https://eatsmartmovemoreva.org/what-is-self-care-tips-and-practices/#:~:text=In%20 fact%2C%20according%20to%20the,relationships%2C%20and%20recover%20from%20 setbacks. on August 16, 2023.

Engle, P. (n.d.). *5 tips for substitute teachers in high school classrooms* [Blog post]. Accessed at https://ess.com/blog/articles-tips-for-substitute-teacher-high-school on May 2, 2023.

Fisher, D., & Frey, N. (2014). *Better learning through structured teaching: A framework for the gradual release of responsibility*. Alexandria, VA: ASCD.

Gillyard, A. (2016, November 1). *3 ways lesson plans flop—and how to recover* [Blog post]. Accessed at www.edutopia.org/blog/3-ways-lesson-plans-flop-how-to-recover-anne-gillyard on January 26, 2023.

Goodreads. (n.d.a). *Jane Goodall quotes*. Accessed at https://goodreads.com/quotes/159740 -what-you-do-makes-a-difference-and-you-have-to on October 27, 2023.

Goodreads. (n.d.b). *Maya Angelou quotes.* Accessed at https://goodreads.com/quotes/7273813-do-the-best-you-can-until-you-know-better-then on August 15, 2023.

Greenwald, A., & Taylor, S. (2022, January 20). What are classroom management tips for substitute teachers? *Nevada Today.* Accessed at www.unr.edu/nevada-today/news/2022/atp-classroom-management-substitute-teacher on January 29, 2023.

Hammond, Z. (2015). *Culturally responsive teaching and the brain: Promoting authentic engagement and rigor among culturally and linguistically diverse students.* Thousand Oaks, CA: Corwin Press.

Harlacher, J. E. (2015). *Designing effective classroom management.* Bloomington, IN: Marzano Resources.

Harvard Health Publishing. (2022, August 25). *5 surprising benefits of walking.* Accessed at www.health.harvard.edu/staying-healthy/5-surprising-benefits-of-walking on July 25, 2023.

Hattie, J. (2023). *Visible learning: The sequel—A synthesis of over 2,100 meta-analyses relating to achievement* (2nd ed.). New York, NY: Routledge.

Heine, A. (2023). *10 reasons why soft skills are important for your career.* Accessed at https://indeed.com/career-advice/interviewing/why-are-soft-skills-important on August 14, 2023.

Killian, S., (2015) *8 strategies Robert Marzano and John Hattie agree on.* Accessed at https://vtss-ric.vcu.edu/media/vtss-ric/documents/s2s-strand-2/2021-2022-session-a-non-accessible/session-b-accessible/quality-core-instructions/VCU-3396_02aag_8StrategiesRobertMarzanoandJohnHattieAgreeOnR1V2.pdf on August 14, 2023.

KnowledgeHut. (2023, July 13). *10 reasons why soft skills are important* [Blog post]. Accessed at https://knowledgehut.com/blog/others/soft-skills-and-its-importance on August 16, 2023.

Lalagos, N. (2023, July 6). *4 key relationships to nurture in your middle or high school classroom.* Accessed at https://edutopia.org/article/nurturing-positive-relationships-school on August 14, 2023.

Lemov, D. (2015). *Teach like a champion 2.0: 62 Techniques that put students on the path to college.* San Francisco: Jossey-Bass.

Marzano, R. J. (2017). *The new art and science of teaching.* Bloomington, IN: Solution Tree Press.

Marzano, R. J., Pickering, D. J., & Pollock, J. E. (2001*). Classroom instruction that works: Research-based strategies for increasing student achievement.* Alexandria, VA: ASCD.

Marzano, R. J., & Pickering, D. J. (2011). *The highly engaged classroom.* Bloomington, IN: Marzano Resources.

Maslow, A. H. (1966). *The psychology of science: A reconnaissance.* New York: Harper & Row.

Mattie, S. (n.d.). *How to become a substitute teacher.* Accessed at www.educationdegree.com/articles/how-to-become-a-substitute-teacher/#easyNavTitle-6 on June 19, 2023.

Mental Health First Aid USA (2022, March 14). *How and why to practice self-care.* Accessed at www.mentalhealthfirstaid.org/2022/03/how-and-why-to-practice-self-care on July 23, 2023.

Müller, C., Otto, B., Sawitzki, V., Kanagalingam, P., Scherer, J.-S., & Lindberg, S. (2021). Short breaks at school: Effects of physical activity and a mindfulness intervention on children's attention, reading comprehension, and self-esteem. *Trends in Neuroscience and Education, 25*(100160). Accessed at https://doi.org/10.1016/j.tine.2021.100160 on October 27, 2023.

Perlow, L. A., & Porter, J. L. (2009). *Making time off predictable—and required.* Accessed at https://hbr.org/2009/10/making-time-off-predictable-and-required on August 16, 2023.

Poulou, M. S. (2017). An examination of the relationship among teachers' perceptions of social-emotional learning, teaching efficacy, teacher-student interactions, and students' behavioral difficulties. *International Journal of School and Educational Psychology, 5*(2), 126–136.

Ramar, K., Malhotra, R. K., Carden, K. A., Martin, J. L., Abbasi-Feinberg, F., Aurora, R. N., et al. (2021). Sleep is essential to health: An American Academy of Sleep Medicine position statement. *Journal of Clinical Sleep Medicine, 17*(10), 2115–2119. Accessed at https://jcsm.aasm.org/doi/10.5664/jcsm.9476 on July 25, 2023.

Reibel, A. R. (2023). *Embracing relational teaching: How strong relationships promote student self-regulation and efficacy.* Bloomington, IN: Solution Tree Press.

Reilly, K. (2021, November 22). *Schools are raising pay and lowering job requirements as they struggle to hire substitute teachers.* Accessed at https://time.com/6121336/substitute-teacher-shortage-pandemic on July 25, 2023.

Scoot Education. (2022, February 25). *Handling challenging student behavior: 5 strategies.* Accessed at https://scoot.education/substitute-teachers/handling-challenging-student-behavior on January 14, 2023.

TeachThought Staff. (2016, March 15). *A teacher makes 1500 educational decisions a day.* Accessed at www.teachthought.com/pedagogy/teacher-makes-1500-decisions-a-day on January 27, 2023.

Terada, Y. (2018, September 11). *Welcoming students with a smile.* Accessed at www.edutopia.org/article/welcoming-students-smile on November 25, 2022.

University of Rochester Medical Center. (2023). *Journaling for emotional wellness.* Accessed at www.urmc.rochester.edu/encyclopedia/content.aspx?ContentID=4552&ContentTypeID=1 on July 25, 2023.

Westring, A. F. (2021, April 20). *There's no "right" way to do self-care.* Accessed at https://hbr.org/2021/04/theres-no-right-way-to-do-self-care on July 25, 2023.

Wu, R. (2022). *6 reasons why having a hobby is important* [Blog post]. Accessed at https://maniology.com/blogs/maniology-blog/why-are-hobbies-important on July 25, 2023.

Index

A
acknowledging each student, 26
acknowledging the regular teacher's absence, 29–30
addressing students who don't meet behavior expectations, 38–39
American Academy of Sleep Medicine, 67
American Psychological Association, 68
Angelou, M., 46
application and employment requirements, 6
appropriateness test, 26
arriving early, 18
article jigsaws, 53
asking for help, 20
  opportunities to learn, 20
avoiding confrontations, 58
avoiding power struggles, 57

B
backup plans
  preparing, 8
  worksheets, 11
  backup lesson ideas, 52–53
  read-aloud books, 8–9
  games, 10–11
Be Glad Your Nose Is on Your Face and Other Poems (Prelutsky), 9
behaviors. *See* student behaviors
being a successful classroom manager, 33–35
  getting students' attention, 37–38
  management by movement, 37
  possible rewards, 35–36
being present in the work, 26–27
being vulnerable vs. a pushover, 24

Better Learning Through Structured Teaching (Fisher & Frey), 40, 84
The Biggest Burp Ever (Nesbitt), 9
Bingham, K., 9
brain breaks, 8
  incorporating, 28–29, 55
brainteasers, 28
buddy teachers, 39
building rapport and trust, 24
  acknowledging each student, 26
  being present, 26–27
  letting your students get to know you, 25
  meet and greet, 24–25
  sharing your experiences, 26
  using appropriate humor, 25–26
business cards, 8, 19

C
callbacks, 37–38
calling the classroom teacher, 13
Campbell, R., 9
carousels, 53
Center for Teaching Innovations, 28
center rotations, 4
  free-time center, 42–43
  in small groups, 42–43
  literacy center, 42
  math center, 42
certification. *See* licensing or certification
chalk talk, 53, 55
Chamorro-Premuzic, T., 66
checking in with the office, 18–19
checking out in the office, 63
  do's and don'ts, 64
checking out the room, 19
check-out protocol, 4

Classroom Instruction That Works (Marzano et al.), 41
classroom management, 3–4
  addressing students who don't meet behavior expectations, 38–39
  being successful, 33–38
  establishing instructional structures, 40–43
  key points, 33
  notes and reflection, 47
  recording your learning, 46
  seeking out instructional resources, 46
  speaking from experience, 46
  using strategies for success, 43–45
Cleary, B., 9
collaborative learning, 40
collaborative teamwork, 4
communicating, 1
  with the classroom teacher, 4
The Complete Nonsense Book (Lear), 9
completing the credential process, 4
connecting with students, 3
  acknowledging the regular teacher's absence, 29–30
  being vulnerable vs. a pushover, 24
  brain breaks, 28
  building rapport and trust, 24–27
  creating a collaborative atmosphere, 28
  inclusion and respect, 29
  key points, 23
  notes and reflection, 31
  speaking from experience, 28
  transitions and routines, 27–28

| 89

connecting with teaching neighbors, 19
cooperative groups, 41–42
    assigning roles, 41
cover letter. *See* sample résumé and cover letter
COVID-19 pandemic
    teaching credentials changes, 76
creating a circle of support, 68
creating a collaborative atmosphere, 28
Cronin, D., 9
Cult of Pedagogy, 12
Cybrary Man's Educational Web Sites, 82

D

Dear Zoo (Campbell), 9
de-escalating a situation, 56–57
Designing Effective Classroom Management (Harlacher), 84
Diary of a Fly (Cronin), 9
diverting challenging behavior, 56
dressing professionally, 17–18

E

Education World, 46, 83
Education.com, 11
Edutopia, 12, 83
Elizabeth, S., 9
Embracing Relational Teaching (Reibel), 83–84
empathy, 1
employment requirements. *See* application and employment requirements
ending strong, 4
    caring for yourself, 64–69
    checking out in the office, 63–64
    end-of-day report form, 62, 70–71
    key points, 61
    leaving a note for the teacher, 62–63
    notes and reflection, 70
    reflecting on what you've learned, 61
    speaking from experience, 69
    tidying the classroom, 61–62
enjoying the ride, 84
establishing instructional structures, 40
    center rotations in small groups, 42–43
    cooperative groups, 41–42
    full-class instruction, 40–41
    independent work, 43
    partner work, 43
exercise, 68
expanding to full-time teaching, 4
expectations
    making clear, 56
    setting, 3–4

F

Falling Up (Silverstein), 9
finding your self-care routine, 65–66
    creating a circle of support, 68
    getting enough sleep, 67
    journaling, 67
    making time to rest and renew, 66–67
Fisher, D., 40, 84
flexibility, 2
focus on growth, 1
focused instruction, 40
following the lesson plan, 43–44, 46
forgiving, 1
Free Educational Resources, 46
Free Technology for Teachers, 12
free-time centers, 42–43
Frey, N., 40, 84
full-class instruction, 40–41
    collaborative learning, 40
    focused instruction, 40
    guided instruction, 40
    independent learning, 40
full-class rewards, 36

G

gallery walks, 53
games
    draw a picture, 10
    rock, paper, scissors, 28
    silent ball, 10–11
    telephone, 10
    thumb wars, 28
    twenty questions, 10
    would you rather? 11, 28
getting enough sleep, 67
getting ready for the job, 5
    application and employment requirements, 6
    licensing or certification, 6
    the specifics, 7
getting ready for the requests, 12
    calling the teacher, 13
    learning about the assignment, 12–13
    planning your preparation, 13–15
getting ready to greet your students, 19
getting students attention, 37–38
getting your game face on, 19
getting your teaching credentials, 75–76
Go Noodle, 83
going and growing, 81–82
    enjoying the ride, 84
    key points, 81
    resources to keep learning, 82–84
    soft skills count, 82
good questions, 44–45
Goodreads, 8
Google folders, 8
Google Forms, 15
Green, D., 9
greeting your students, 24–25
guest teachers, 1–2
    increased pay, 1
    mindset, 2
guided instruction, 40
guided stretch or movement activities, 28–29

H

Harlacher, J. E., 84
Harris, C., 9
Hernandez, J., 84
The Highly Engaged Classroom (Marzano & Pickering), 84
How to Draw 101 Animals (Green), 9
How to Draw 101 Cute Stuff for Kids (Elizabeth), 9
human resources. *See* using your human resources
humor. *See* using appropriate humor

I

I Did Awesome Today! form, 36, 48
I'm Just No Good at Rhyming (Harris), 9
immunizations, 7
inclusion and respect, 29
independent work, 40, 43
instructional resources, 46
instructional structures, 3–4, 46
Ish (Reynolds), 9

J

journaling, 67
"Journaling for Mental Health" (University of Rochester Medical Center), 67

K

K5 Learning, 11
Kahoot! 11, 83
keeping calm, 39
    key points, 51
    notes and reflection, 59
    reflecting on challenging experiences, 58
    respond instead of react, 51–57

Index

speaking from experience, 58
keeping calm, 4
key points
    classroom management, 33
    connecting with students, 23
    ending strong, 61
    going and growing, 81
    keeping calm, 51
    next steps, 73
    preparing for success, 5
    staring out strong, 17
Khan Academy, 83
Kim, J., 84

L
Lear, E., 9
learning about the assignment, 12–13
leaving a note for the teacher, 62
    end-of-the-day report form, 71
    sample, 63
Lee, S., 66
Lemov, D., 84
lesson savers, 55
letting students get to know you, 25
licensing or certification, 6
    getting your credentials, 75–76
A Light in the Attic (Silverstein), 9
literacy centers, 42
long-term substitute teaching, 74–75

M
management by movement, 37
Martin's Big Words (Rappaport), 9
Marzano, R. J., 41, 83–84
Maslow, A. H., 82
mathematics centers, 42
meet and greet, 24–25
must do's and may do's, 44
My Perfect Resume, 77

N
name-calling, 58
National Council for Mental Well-Being, 65
National Sleep Foundation, 67
Nesbitt, K., 9
The New Art and Science of Teaching (Marzano), 83
next steps, 73
    getting your credentials, 75–76
    key points, 73
    long-term substitute teaching, 74–75
    notes and reflection, 79
    preparation activities, 73–74
    sample résumé and cover letter, 77–78
    speaking from experience, 76

notes and reflection
    classroom management, 47
    connecting with students, 31
    ending strong, 70
    keeping calm, 59
    next steps, 79
    preparing for success, 16
    starting out strong, 21
nurturing hobbies and interests, 68

O
Oops, I Didn't Make a Good Decision Today form, 39, 50, 62
organizational tips, 3
Owl Moon (Yolen), 9

P
paperwork requirements, 3
Parent Portfolio, 11
partner work, 43
Perlow, L. A., 68
personal care items, 8
physical self-care, 68
Pickering, D. J., 41, 84
picking your battles, 54
Pinterest, 12
planning your preparation, 13–15
    assignment notes template, 14
Pollack, J. E., 41
Porter, J. L., 68
positivity, 2
poster summaries, 53, 55
power struggles, 57
practice problems, 52
praising, 35, 46
Prelutsky, J., 9
preparing for next steps, 74–75
preparing for success, 3
    key points, 5
    speaking from experience, 15
    notes and reflection, 16
    getting ready for the job, 5–7
    creating a survival kit, 7–8
    preparing backup plans, 8–11
    using your human resources, 11–12
    getting ready for the requests, 12–15
professional development, 4, 74

Q
questions, 3
    for students, 34, 44–45
    long-term substitute teaching, 74–75
    students writing, 53
    to ask about the assignment, 12
    to ask the classroom teacher, 13

Quizlet, 83

R
Ramar, K., 67
Ramona the Pest (Cleary), 9
Rappaport, D., 9
read-aloud books, 8–9
ReadWorks, 42, 46
reciprocity, 76
recording your learning, 46
redirecting negative behaviors, 57
re-engaging students, 4
reflecting
    on challenging experiences, 58
    on what you've learned, 61
regrouping, 4
Reibel, A. R., 83–84
Reilly, K., 1
relational teaching, 83–84
resources, 82–84
respect, 1, 29
responding instead of reacting, 51–52
    when concrete plans are lacking, 52–53
    when plans are unsuccessful or have glitches, 53–54
    when student behaviors derail the lesson, 54–58
rest and renewal, 66–67
Resume Builder, 77
résumé. *See* sample résumé and cover letter
rewards, 35–36
    full-class, 36
    table or team, 36
Reynolds, P. H., 9
routines. *See* transitions and routines
rudeness, 58

S
sage on the stage, 28
sample résumé and cover letter, 4, 77–78
    keeping up-to0date, 7
"The Science of Resting (Well)," (Chamorro–Premuzic & Lee), 66
seating charts, 46
self-care, 4, 64–65, 81
    finding your own routine, 65–68
    nurturing hobbies and interests, 69
    physical, 68
    start fresh every day, 69
    taking time off, 68
setting expectations, 3–4
setting the stage, 3
sharing your experiences, 26

Silverstein, S., 9
sleep. *See* getting enough sleep
small-group work, 4
soft skills count, 82
songs playlist, 27
speaking from experience
    classroom management, 46
    connecting with students, 28
    ending strong, 69
    keeping calm, 58
    keeping up-to-date, 74
    next steps, 76
    preparing for success, 15
    starting out strong, 20
specifics, 7
starting fresh every day, 69
starting out strong, 3
    arriving early, 18
    asking for help, 20
    checking in with the office, 18–19
    checking out the room, 19
    connecting with teaching neighbors, 19
    dressing professionally, 17–18
    getting ready to greet your students, 19
    key points, 17
    notes and reflection, 21
    opportunities to learn, 20
    speaking from experience, 20
station rotations. *See* center rotations
Storyboard That, 83
student behaviors, 4
    diverting challenging, 56
    redirecting, 57
    setting expectations, 33–38
    when students don't meet expectations, 38–39
    when they derail the lesson plan, 54–56
students writing quiz questions, 53
substitute assignment notes template, 14
substitute teachers. *See* guest teachers
Substitute Teaching from A to Z, 46
Super Star awards, 36, 49
Super Teacher Worksheets, 11
supportive interactions, 3
survival kits
    business cards, 8
    creating, 3, 7
    personal care items, 8
    teaching supplies, 8
    using, 43–44

T

table or team rewards, 36
taking time off, 68
Teach Like a Champion Field Guide 2.0 (Lemov et al.), 84
Teacher Certification Degrees, 76
Teacher Vision, 46, 83
teacher-student relationships. *See* connecting with students
TeachHUB, 12
The Teaching Channel, 83
teaching supplies, 8
TeachThought, 12
team challenges, 52
team summary/brainstorming, 52
TedEd, 83
ThoughtCo, 46
tidying up the classroom, 61–62
Time Management, 1 (no author)
tips from teachers. *See* speaking from experience

transitions and routines, 27–28
    planning, 27
trust, 23

U

University of Rochester Medical Center, 67
using appropriate humor, 25–26
using strategies for success, 43–44
    good questions, 44–45
    must do's and may do's, 44
using your human resources, 11–12

W

Westring, A. F., 65
when concrete plans are lacking, 52
    backup lesson ideas, 52–53
when plans are unsuccessful or have glitches, 53–54
    four Rs, 54
    lesson savers, 55
when student behaviors derail the lesson, 54–56
    avoiding power struggles, 57
    diverting challenging behavior, 56
    redirecting negative behaviors, 57
    using language to de-escalate, 56–57
Where the Sidewalk Ends (Silverstein), 9
whole group activities, 28
whole-class instruction, 4
worksheets, 11
Wu, R., 69

Y

Yolen, J., 9

Z

Z Is for Moose! (Bingham), 9
Zety, 77

Thriving as a New Teacher
John F. Eller and Sheila A. Eller
Discover strategies and tools for new-teacher success. Explore the six critical areas related to teaching that most impact new teachers and their students, from understanding yourself and implementing effective assessments to working confidently and effectively with colleagues.
BKF661

Owning It
Alex Kajitani
Today's fast-changing culture presents a great challenge—and a great opportunity—in schools and in the teaching profession. With Owning It, you will discover an array of easy-to-implement strategies designed to help you excel in your classroom, at your school, and in your community.
BKF835

The Beginning Teacher's Field Guide
Tina H. Boogren
The joys and pains of starting a teaching career often go undiscussed. This guide explores the personal side of teaching, offering crucial advice and support. The author details six phases every new teacher goes through and outlines classroom strategies and self-care practices.
BKF806

Take Time for You
Tina H. Boogren
The key to thriving as a human and an educator rests in self-care. With *Take Time for You*, you'll discover a clear path to well-being. The author offers manageable strategies, reflection questions, and surveys that will guide you in developing an individualized self-care plan.
BKF813

Solution Tree | Press

Visit SolutionTree.com or call 800.733.6786 to order.

"Tremendous, tremendous, tremendous!

The speaker made me do some very deep internal reflection about the **PLC process** and the personal responsibility I have in making the school improvement process work for **ALL kids**."

—Marc Rodriguez, teacher effectiveness coach, Denver Public Schools, Colorado

PD Services

Our experts draw from decades of research and their own experiences to bring you practical strategies for building and sustaining a high-performing PLC. You can choose from a range of customizable services, from a one-day overview to a multiyear process.

Book your PLC PD today!
888.763.9045

Solution Tree